Beverley Sutherland Smith's

Delicious Desserts

The Five Mile Press
P.O. Box 327
Poole
Dorset BH15 2RG
United Kingdom

First published 1989

First published in the UK 1990

Design by Greg Mason

Typeset by Southern Cross Typesetting, Keysborough.
Printed in Singapore by Kyodo Printing Co. Ltd.

Cataloguing-in-Publication data

Smith, Beverley Sutherland.
Delicious desserts.

Includes index.
ISBN 0 86788 185 2.

1. Desserts. I. Title.

641.8′6

Cover Photograph: Apple Blossoms (page 16).

Beverley Sutherland Smith's

Delicious Desserts

For Every Occasion

The Five Mile Press

IN PRAISE OF DESSERT

I have always had a great fondness for desserts, but I'm sometimes made to feel guilty when those with more self-discipline wave their hands in refusal at the end of a meal. Yet, for me, desserts must be beautiful or I can't be bothered making or eating them. I call a bowl of perfect ripe raspberries beautiful — nestling in a few dewy green leaves, with a jug of thick cream alongside. I love a scoop of ice-cream, full of intense flavour, creamy yet light, perhaps decorated with just a single frosted flower, a flaky roll of chocolate or a glazed nut, and served in a wine glass. And, in summer, there's nothing like a fruit tart, the pastry crisp, the warm filling spilling its juices onto plates to be scooped up with a generous spoon.

Desserts are so often seasonal delights, richly coloured and flavoured according to what is available. Some may be delicate and elegant, others hearty and rustic, yet all desserts should be a joyous affair.

Putting together this collection involved serious thought as to what kind of recipes to include: elaborate, creative ones, using exotic flavourings, such as elderberry, roses, rare liqueurs or spun sugar and last-minute preparation, or ones which would have imaginative and mouth-watering ideas but would be highly useable. Of course, it had to be the latter; this book is not meant for professionals but for those of you who simply enjoy cooking and eating, and sharing these occasions with others.

Included here are some nostalgic dishes (which, sadly, are sometimes forgotten), light and fruity sweets, hot and cold puddings, tarts and ice-creams. While some may take more time than others, none is really difficult. Many can be prepared days ahead.

It matters little what you have chosen as a main dish, a dessert can be found here to complement it. I have compiled the following guide to help you find the right dessert for the occasion.

It hardly seems necessary to tell you to use only the best of all ingredients for desserts, but be sure that you do. This will make such a difference to the texture, aroma and, most of all, the taste. For me, dessert is an important part of any special meal, whether it's a family affair or a formal occasion. After all the last taste will be the memory that lingers.

Beverley Sutherland Smith
Melbourne, 1989.

Contents

MEASUREMENTS

Standard measuring cups and spoons
are used in this book. All cup
and spoon measurements are
level at the rim.

Large eggs (67g/2 ¼ oz) have been
used in testing these recipes.

It is important to consistently follow
either Imperial or Metric measurements
in each recipe.

WHAT TO SERVE WHEN

A Quick Reference Guide.

After a Light Main Course

After an Oriental-style Meal

After a Rich Main Course

Barbecue Desserts

*Catering for a Crowd**

*These recipes can easily be doubled.

Children's Desserts

Decadent Desserts

Family Favourites

Healthy Eating

Picnic Desserts

Quick and Easy

Special Occasions

Cold Fruit Desserts

Fresh fruits give us the best of both worlds: the joy of tasting seasonal fruits, and the knowledge that they are good for us. As English food writer Jane Grigson comments in *Jane Grigson's Fruit Book:* 'This special feeling towards fruit, its glory and abundance is, I would say, universal. We have to bear the burden of it being good for us.'

Flavours, textures and the beauty of fruits have been the inspiration of writers for centuries. I have read descriptions of lemons as 'edible sunshine'; strawberries as 'all summer in a china bowl'; and, according to a Japanese poet, a peach is 'the left cheek of my girl'.

When you buy fresh fruit to serve after a meal, it should be as perfect in every way as possible. You can cheat a little when fruit is to be cooked; it can be trimmed, and syrup can be added to give more flavour. I don't have much time for out-of-season fruits, except as a garnish or combined with fruits which are in season. Out-of-season fruits are usually tasteless, even when they look perfect.

Pears in Rhubarb and Red Wine

A big bowl of deep, burgundy-coloured pears cooked in red wine is a lovely sweet which keeps well. In fact, the pears improve if they are left to steep in the syrup for days, being turned over occasionally if there is not enough syrup to keep them moist. With stalks of rhubarb added, the colour is even prettier and the flavour tart, yet elusive. Pile them up on a shallow bowl, stalks uppermost, and surrounded by the vivid juices and put some thick running cream in a jug on the table.

6 pears

1 cup (8 fl oz) red wine

1 cup sugar

1 cup (8 fl oz) water

1 cinnamon stick about 5 cm (2") in length

3 or 4 strips orange rind

2 long stalks rhubarb (4 if you're using the baby spring rhubarb)

Peel the pears, but leave their stalks on. Heat the wine, sugar, water with cinnamon stick and orange rind in a saucepan and, when it comes to the boil, add the rhubarb and pears. If the pears are not covered by liquid — you need to use a pan in which they will fit snugly — turn them over when placing them in the liquid so the outsides are moist. Turn over several times while they are cooking.

Cover the pan and simmer very gently until the pears are quite tender. Test with the point of a very small sharp knife or fine poultry skewer. Remove the pears and pour the liquid through a strainer. Don't push the rhubarb through or you will have fibrous bits in the sauce, but press down to get all the juices into the sauce.

If you think the syrup is too thin you can boil it rapidly to thicken, but be sure to leave plenty of liquid so the pears will be moist when they are stored. Chill and leave a day before eating, or keep for 4 to 5 days, turning the pears over each day if any are out of the syrup.

Serves 6

SUMMER FRUITS IN CREAMY RASPBERRY SAUCE

Strawberries and cream, raspberries and cream — these are the simplest yet loveliest ways to serve these summer fruits. This is a variation on the theme. Rosewater lends a perfumed air to a kirsch-flavoured cream, which softly coats the fruit.

1 punnet (250 g/8 oz) raspberries
1 punnet (250 g/8 oz) strawberries
1 punnet (250 g/8 oz) either blueberries, blackberries or youngberries
2 tbsp sugar
1 tbsp kirsch
few drops rosewater
3 tbsp thick cream

Take out about a third of the punnet of raspberries and place in a bowl. Sprinkle with sugar, kirsch and rosewater and leave to stand for about an hour.

Push through a sieve so you have a bright crimson juice without any of the pips. Chill this. It is best added to the berries just before dinner.

Mix the remainder of the raspberries with the hulled strawberries and blueberries, blackberries or youngberries, and chill.

When you are ready to assemble the dessert, mix the cream into the berry sauce and taste. If it is too tart, a little more sugar could be added, but at this stage it is best to add icing sugar. Stir the creamy sauce very gently into the mixed berries and tip it into either the prettiest large crystal bowl you have, or into individual dishes.

Don't serve any extra cream with this, just some almond wafers (page 129) alongside, or a platter of madeleines (page 128).

Serves 6

Compote of Fruits of Summer

This is a dish which can be varied according to what fruits are in season, but you need to have at least 4 different types to make it really interesting. If you can get them, try nectarines. They lend a soft pink tinge to the fruit, or use red plums for a vivid colour.

The fruit is cooked separately, because some fruits take longer than others. This is not much trouble, and the compote keeps beautifully. In fact, it improves if left several days.

1½ cups (12 fl oz) water
¾ cup sugar
4 small plums
2 nectarines
2 yellow peaches
2 large oranges
90 g (3 oz) seedless grapes
1 punnet (250 g/8 oz) blackberries, youngberries or blueberries
1 tbsp kirsch or brandy

Heat the water and sugar together until there are no sugar granules in the pan. Cut the plums into quarters, remove the stones, and add the fruit to the syrup. Simmer gently (uncovered) until tender and remove with a slotted spoon to a bowl. Cut the nectarines and peaches into quarters and add to the syrup. Again simmer until tender and remove with the spoon to the plums.

Peel the oranges and remove all the white pith. Cut the oranges into segments and add with the grapes to the hot syrup. Leave for only about a minute. Remove to the bowl, and let the syrup cool. Add the kirsch or brandy and pour over the top. There should be plenty of syrup for this compote. If the fruit is very firm and you need to cook for some time, place a lid on the pan while cooking. (Otherwise the syrup may reduce too much.) Add the berries and chill.

Serves 8

A selection of ice-creams: cherry (page 34), peach (page 35) and passionfruit (page 36).

Peaches in a Crimson Jelly (page 7).

PINEAPPLE SLICES WITH CARDAMON SEEDS

After saffron, cardamon is one of the most expensive spices in the world, with an aromatic flavour linked with the spiciness of ginger. There are three varieties, but the one most commonly found is the plump whitish pod. For flavouring fruit or a dessert, you need to remove the pod and crush the seeds lightly. They are not difficult to break and, freshly prepared, will release all the spicy aroma. You can't use the powdered cardamon, it really doesn't have anything like the flavour needed for this dish.

1 small – medium-sized ripe pineapple
12 whole cardamon seeds, pods removed
piece cinnamon stick, about 2.5 cm (1" in length)
½ cup (4 fl oz) water
1 tbsp sugar
12 pistachio nuts

Cut the top and bottom from the pineapple. Peel the skin, cutting fairly deeply so you remove the brown 'eyes'. If any remain, remove them. Cut the pineapple into thinnish slices and place into a bowl.

Crush the cardamon seeds, using a rolling pin or a pestle and mortar. Then put them into a small saucepan, adding the cinnamon stick, water and sugar. Bring to the boil. Turn off the heat, cover the saucepan, and leave the mixture to steep for about 15 minutes. Remove the cinnamon stick and pour the mixture over the pineapple. Chill and leave at least 8 hours for the flavours of the syrup to blend into the fruit before serving.

Blanch the pistachio nuts in water. Remove the dark skin and cut the nuts into thin slices. Arrange the pineapple slices on individual plates and scatter slivers of nut over the top.

Serves 6

Caramel oranges

You don't find this dessert on menus as often as you once did but, prepared with a caramel coating, these oranges make up a lovely refreshing dish that shouldn't be forgotten. A good choice after a rich dinner, it is easy and inexpensive.

6 oranges
1 cup sugar
½ cup (4 fl oz) water
an additional ½ cup (4 fl oz) water

Remove the rind from 2 of the oranges with a zester or vegetable peeler and cut into very fine shreds. Place them into cold water and cook until they are quite tender. Peel all the oranges, removing every trace of white pith. Slice each one across horizontally and reassemble in their original shape in individual serving bowls. You can use a tooth-pick to keep them in place. Keep the slices thin or this is an awkward dish to eat.

Heat the sugar and water gently until the sugar has dissolved. Turn up the heat and cook to a rich golden brown caramel. Don't stir at any stage, as this can make the sugar crystallise. Add the additional water. It will splatter furiously, so cover your hand with a piece of cloth to hold the pan handle. Return to the heat and warm again to dissolve any lumpy bits of caramel. Leave to cool until tepid and glaze the oranges with the caramel, spooning over the top. Keep aside ½ cup for cooking the rind.

Chill the oranges thoroughly. The caramel becomes thinner with the juices from the orange, so don't keep longer than 8 hours. Cook the blanched orange rind strips in the retained ½ cup of caramel until they are very glazed and firmly candied. Take them out and spread on a little piece of oiled foil to keep them separate. Just before serving, scatter the wisps of orange peel over the top of each orange.

Serves 6

Apricots poached in apple juice

The flavour is so intense you need only eat small portions of this dessert. It is a lovely reminder of summer apricots during winter months, when the choice of fruit is limited and yet you want to serve something fruity.

It is much nicer if vanilla pod (rather than essence) is used in the syrup to get a true flavour and perfume. If you don't use the pod, flavour with a little vanilla essence when the apricots are cool.

185 g (6 oz) dried apricots
3 strips orange peel
3 strips lemon peel
2 cups (16 fl oz) pure apple juice
½ vanilla pod
½ cup sugar

Place the apricots with orange and lemon peel into a saucepan and add the apple juice. Cut the vanilla pod lengthwise to expose the seeds, and add. Warm the apple juice, add the sugar and cover the pan. Simmer very gently until the apricots are tender. It usually takes about 20 minutes.

Remove the apricots with a slotted spoon to a bowl and take out the vanilla bean. Scrape out the dark soft section and return this to the syrup. Boil rapidly for a couple of minutes; you just need to thicken the syrup slightly, but be careful not to reduce too much as the fruit needs a generous amount around it.

Pour over the apricots. (You can leave in the orange peel.) When the fruit is cool, chill. This keeps beautifully for about a week.

Serves 6

PEACHES IN A CRIMSON JELLY

A vivid dish in both colour and flavour, fresh raspberries stain the champagne a deep crimson and are set with halves of poached peaches, their graceful yellow curves breaking gently through the jelly.

4 yellow peaches
1 cup (8 fl oz) champagne
½ cup (4 fl oz) water
½ cup sugar
strip of vanilla bean, about 5 cm (2") in length
125 g (4 oz) fresh raspberries
2 tsp gelatine
1 tbsp water

Peel the peaches and halve them, removing the stones. Heat the champagne, water, sugar and vanilla bean in a saucepan. When the sugar has dissolved, add the peaches and poach very gently until they are tender. Remove and place in a bowl with the cut side down. Add the raspberries to the liquid and bring to the boil. Remove from the heat and leave to steep for about 10 minutes.

Mix the gelatine with water, add to the raspberry peach syrup, and then pour the mixture through a sieve over the peaches in the bowl. Don't press down too hard — you want to avoid getting seeds in the liquid — although you can push lightly with the back of a spoon to be sure all the red juices come through.

Chill until set. It should be covered with plastic wrap once cold.

Serves 4

Melon Balls in an Apricot Sauce

In this recipe, melon balls are left to steep in a sauce made from orange and dried apricots. This dessert, a glowing apricot-colour, is most refreshing. It must be served chilled.

1 large rockmelon (cantaloup) or 2 smaller ones
½ cup (4 fl oz) orange juice
4 dried apricots
2 tbsp sugar

Cut the rockmelon into halves, scrape out the seeds and, using a melon baller, scoop out neat balls. Place these in a bowl. There is always some wastage when you do this. You can use the scraps for a family dish of fruit salad or purée them and freeze with sugar to make a frozen fruity sorbet.

Put the orange juice and apricots into a saucepan. Leave to stand for 10 minutes to soften the dried fruit, then heat gently and cook until softened. Be careful not to let all the liquid boil away. If it is reducing too much, cover the saucepan. Mix in the sugar when the mixture is soft, and purée in a blender. Leave to cool. Taste it. If it doesn't taste fresh and is only slightly tart, you can add a teaspoon of lemon juice. The flavour depends very much on the oranges. Pour over the rockmelon, stir gently and chill for at least 4 hours.

A dish which is best without any cream, I like it just as it is. But I find some people enjoy a scoop of vanilla ice-cream on the side.

Serves 4

Fruit salad

This is only a guideline. Choose fruits with an eye for freshness and compatible flavour and for attractive colour combinations. It is best to have only three fruits, if they are the best in season, rather than a huge range. Keep fruit in larger pieces so each mouthful is recognisable.

The salad is made with a syrup, tart-flavoured and coloured to a translucent deep pink with juices from raspberries. If you can't buy fresh ones, frozen berries will do very well instead.

½ cup (4 fl oz) water
¼ cup sugar
125 g (4 oz) raspberries
2 oranges
1 punnet (250 g/8 oz) strawberries
125 g (4 oz) seedless grapes
3 kiwi fruit
6 slices pineapple

Put the water and sugar into a saucepan and cook until syrupy. Add the raspberries while hot and remove from the heat. Leave to steep for about 30 minutes and pour through a sieve, pressing down to get as much as possible of the raspberry juices through. If you don't want to prepare the fruit salad immediately, this can be stored several days in the refrigerator.

Remove the skin from the oranges and all of the white pith and take out the segments with a sharp knife. Put the oranges into a bowl.

Hull berries and add with grapes, peeled, sliced kiwi fruit and the pineapple (its core removed and the flesh cut into chunky pieces).

Pour the syrup over the top, stir or toss gently and refrigerate several hours or until chilled. Don't leave longer than 4 hours or the fruit will soften too much.

Serves 6

Apple orange jelly

An especially good jellied dessert for occasions when you haven't got much time. Be sure to use freshly-squeezed orange juice for a fresh flavour, and buy pure apple juice, not apple juice drink (which is too diluted). Instead of layering the fruit jelly with orange slices it can be made more simply by pouring the jelly into a large bowl or individual dishes, topping when set with segments of fresh orange.

1 cup (8 fl oz) orange juice
1 cup (8 fl oz) apple juice
1 tbsp gelatine
⅓ cup sugar
2 large oranges

Mix the orange and apple juices together. Add about ¾ cup of this to the gelatine and mix well. Put into a small saucepan and add the sugar. Warm gently until the sugar and gelatine have dissolved.

Stir in the remaining juices and pour three-quarters of the jelly into dessert dishes, or you could use shallow cup-shaped champagne glasses.

Cut the peel from the oranges, taking away every scrap of white pith. Cut into halves and then cut each orange into very thin slices, discarding any seeds. When the jelly has almost set, cover with a layer of orange and then pour in the rest of the jelly to make a coating. Chill completely.

It can be served plain or with a jug of cream.

Serves 4

ORIENTAL MANGOES

This fruit has the most wonderful flavour. Juicy and fragrant, it's unnecessary to do anything much with a mango except choose it perfectly ripe. The colour can be misleading, rely on the feel. They should be evenly soft to the touch and without any brown spots on the skin. Serve only slightly chilled, not too intensely cold. When cut the oriental way, the mango looks very pretty, and it is easy to eat the cubes of flesh from the skin. A note of warning: some varieties of mango are very fibrous around the stone. If you cut too close it will give a ragged finish. However, it only requires a little practice to perfect the oriental-style cutting of the mango. The first one or two may be a bit lopsided, but you can keep the most successful ones for your special guests.

6 ripe mangoes

Chill the mango first, as it should only be cut close to serving time.

Place each one upright on a board. Cut vertically (each side of the stone, and as close to the stone as possible), as if you were cutting two thick outside slices. Cut right through, separating the two outside sections from the stone and clinging inner flesh.

Using a sharp knife, score the flesh of the two halves into diamond-shaped cubes, making sure you don't cut right through to the skin. Take each half and turn the skin inside out. The flesh will open up in easily separated diamonds.

Place on a platter. They look lovely on some green leaves. If they are small you will need to allow a whole mango per person. There is a certain amount of wastage when cutting this way because you can't go too close to the stone or the mango will be ragged.

I like mangoes plain, but have eaten them prepared this way and then sprinkled with a tiny spoonful of galiano or curacao. This was also very good.

Serves 3

CHOCOLATE-COATED PINEAPPLE MOULD

This pineapple dessert is quite a simple, fruity jellied mould. It has always been a great demonstration success in my cooking school because of the novel method of coating with chocolate, using a piece of plastic wrap. This effective trick could be used for any moulded dessert.

1 440 g can pineapple pieces
2 tbsp lemon juice
1 tbsp gelatine
¼ cup water
grated rind 1 orange
1 cup (8 fl oz) cream
¾ cup icing sugar (confectioner's sugar)
2 tbsp Grand Marnier

Drain the pineapple. (The juice is not used in the recipe.) Purée the pineapple with lemon juice. Mix the gelatine with the water in a cup over a saucepan of hot water and dissolve. Add to the pineapple, with the orange rind. Mix well and chill until slightly syrupy.

Beat the cream until it holds soft peaks. Add icing sugar and Grand Marnier and fold into the pineapple. Pour into a bowl with a capacity of 4 cups and refrigerate until set. Dip the mould into warm water and turn out onto a plate.

CHOCOLATE COATING

30 g (1 oz) unsalted butter
90 g (3 oz) dark sweetened chocolate
additional whipped cream
a few shreds of orange rind

Chop the butter into a few pieces and break the chocolate into squares. Melt both together in a bowl standing over a saucepan of hot water. Have a piece of plastic wrap spread out flat on your bench, and pour the chocolate into the centre. Spread it out to about the size of a small entrée plate or bread and butter plate, approximately 15 cm (6″) in diameter. If very liquid, leave just a few minutes so it does not run off when you lift up the plastic.

Pat the top of the pineapple filling with some kitchen paper so it will not be wet. Lift the chocolate on the paper and place over the top of the mould. This is not as difficult as it may sound. Press down on the plastic. If it does not cover the mould completely, spread it out with your fingers. The piece of plastic wrap will have little creases in it, but this gives an interesting effect when it is set. Don't worry if it doesn't quite cover the mould.

Chill until set and, if not serving that day, leave the plastic on so the chocolate will remain shining and the mould keep more successfully. It can be left like this for 2 days.

TO SERVE

Gently peel away the plastic, starting at the base. Pipe with whipped cream around the base, which usually looks a bit untidy. Decorate the top with some shreds of orange rind which have been softened by cooking for 5 minutes in a pan of boiling water, or else scatter them around the base with the cream.

When you serve this dessert, a knife dipped in very hot water cuts through the chocolate easily so it doesn't crack or shatter, although the use of butter with the chocolate prevents it becoming too hard.

Serves 6

PEAR MOULD

In *Jane Grigson's Fruit Book*, the author says:

> Pears should be picked first and then ripened in the house. A ripe pear gives very slightly around the stem but should be in no way squashy. All this provides problems for the shopkeeper and supplier. The result is that most people have never eaten a decent pear in their lives.

Pears *are* a difficult fruit. I have discarded more out of my fruit bowl at home than any other fruit; one day not quite ripe enough, the next morning soft and floury.

This dessert gives you the essence of the perfume and flavour without the difficulties of timing your perfect pear; the ones you use just need to be ripe. If their texture is not perfect, it is rarely noticeable in the purée.

This is a more delicious dessert than the ingredients and presentation may indicate. You can try it plain, with the caramel ginger sauce, or some running cream.

1 kg (2 lb) ripe eating pears
3 tbsp lemon juice
125 g (4 oz) sugar
1 tbsp gelatine
⅓ cup (2½ fl oz) water
½ cup (4 fl oz) cream

Peel, core and dice the pears roughly. Mix with the lemon juice and purée in a food processor or put through a moulin. Place a little of the pear purée into a saucepan with the sugar and warm until the sugar has dissolved. Add the remainder of the pear purée and heat until it is tepid. Don't overcook or the taste is not as fresh. Mix the gelatine with the water, dissolve standing in a cup in a pan of hot water. Add to the pears, stir and leave to cool completely.

Whip the cream until it holds very soft peaks. (If it is too firm it won't fold evenly into the pears.) Mix the cream through the purée gently but thoroughly and pour the mixture into a mould which holds about 4 cups. You can use a cake tin, and slice the dessert when serving, or a fancy type of jelly mould.

Chill until set. It only takes a couple of hours. Dip the mould into warm water and invert onto a plate. Cover with plastic wrap if not using within a few hours. It can be made 36 hours ahead.

It looks a bit plain served like this, so you could pipe a few rosettes of cream around the edge to make it appear more exotic.

CARAMEL GINGER SAUCE

1/3 cup (2 1/2 fl oz) water
3/4 cup sugar
additional 1/2 cup (4 fl oz) water
3 tsp grated fresh green ginger

This is very sweet, so use only a spoonful or you will overwhelm the pear flavour. If you have any over it can be stored for about 6 weeks in the refrigerator. Sometimes it thickens too much. If so, a few spoonfuls of boiling water will thin it, or you could warm it again near to dinnertime, and then refrigerate until cool.

Place the water and sugar into a saucepan. Warm until the sugar has dissolved, shaking the pan occasionally. Turn up the heat and boil until a deep golden toffee. Have the water measured out ready, as it must be added instantly to prevent the mixture caramelising too much and becoming too dark. Be careful: it splatters everywhere, so for safety hold the handle of the pan with a towel to prevent any burns. Remove from the heat, add the water and return to the stove, stirring if any bits of hard caramel remain in the base. Cook until bubbling again and add the fresh ginger.

Leave to steep until the syrup is tepid, usually about 20 minutes. Pour through a fine sieve into a jug and refrigerate, lightly covered with some plastic wrap, or store in a jar with a lid.

Serves 8

STRAWBERRIES WITH RHUBARB

Even people who are not rhubarb fans seem to like this dish, perhaps because the strawberry dominates, being just coated with a slightly tart syrup. It's most refreshing, and ideal to follow a rich dinner.

250 g (8 oz) rhubarb
1/2 cup (4 fl oz) orange juice
grated rind 1 orange
1 piece cinnamon stick, about 2.5 cm (1") in length
1/3 cup (2 1/2 oz) sugar or more if the rhubarb is very sour
2 punnets (500 g/1 lb) strawberries

Cut the rhubarb into pieces about 2.5 cm (1") in length. As you do this, pull away any stringy pieces from the stalks. Put the rhubarb into a saucepan with the orange juice, orange rind and cinnamon stick.

Add the sugar and bring gently to the boil. Cover the pan and cook over gentle heat for about 5 minutes. Then check for tenderness. This will depend on the rhubarb, but be careful not to overcook it or the dish will be a stringy mass.

Remove to a bowl, leave to cool and take out the cinnamon stick. Cover and refrigerate. This part of the dessert can be done several days beforehand.

Hull the berries and slice them thickly. Chill. Several hours before serving, put half the berries into a dessert bowl, pour over half the rhubarb, then top with remainder of berries and rhubarb. This is the easiest way to mix them together without having to stir the rhubarb and mash it up. Serve with a jug of thick cream.

Serves 6

ROMANTIC MANGOES

The mango is a most sensual fruit, with its wonderful yellow-to-orange colour and its luscious, juicy flavour. Mangoes seem to have found their way onto my plate on so many romantic occasions — from picnics on the beach and dinners in the light of a tropical moon to champagne breakfasts.

3 ripe mangoes
3 tbsp Grand Marnier
¾ cup plain yoghurt
¾ cup cream, lightly whipped
brown sugar
about 12 amaretti (almond macaroons)

Peel the mangoes and cut the flesh into cubes. Keep aside 6 of the nicest pieces for garnishing. Put a little of the flesh into wine glasses, or shallow champagne glasses. Top each one with a little Grand Marnier.

Mix the cream and yoghurt together and add a spoonful of this to each glass. Top with a scatter of brown sugar and crumbled macaroons. Then add another spoonful of mango, more cream and yoghurt, more brown sugar and macaroons, continuing until you have used them all up. I find I usually get about 3 layers — the top one must be cream.

Decorate with the reserved pieces of mango. Chill 30 minutes for the sugar to melt into a caramel. It tastes wonderful and is so simple to assemble.

Serves 6

Flowers of fig

When soft and perfectly ripe, figs need little preparation. Their skin is very thin so you usually only need to wash them. But, for this dish, I usually peel the figs; you can please yourself whether you do or not. You can use either a purple or green fig, but choose them carefully, ripe but without bruises.

It seems best to serve this fruit whole and in simple ways, so as not to blur the flavour (which you either like or not). This dish enhances the fig mainly by presentation. A little honey syrup is added to give sweetness and a fresh raspberry, placed in the centre of each fig, creates a flower-like effect.

12 ripe figs

½ cup (4 fl oz) water

1 tbsp honey

1 tbsp lemon juice

2 tbsp kirsh

⅓ cup (2½ fl oz) cream

12 perfect raspberries

Heat the water, honey and lemon juice in a saucepan until lightly syrupy. Add the kirsch and leave to cool completely. Mix through the cream, and chill. It can be kept in the refrigerator for 24 hours.

Cut each fig down to make four sections, leaving joined at the base. Open out gently so it looks like a flower. Place a raspberry in the centre. (It will hold the fig open.) Now place the figs, allowing two per person, on either some fig leaves if you are lucky enough to have a tree, or on small green leaves.

Just before serving, trickle a little of the syrup over the centre of each one. If you prefer not to coat the fruit, serve a small puddle of sauce around the base.

Serves 6

Apple blossoms

Adapted from an idea I saw in a French restaurant in Washington, some years ago. The chef had made a sticky apple marmalade and covered the top with berries, for a fresh light dessert. The idea is simple: the sliced strawberries form a petalled design on top of apple purée. You can make the apple up several days in advance, but be warned: it must be very stiff or the base will spread out over the plate, spoiling the appearance. Have the strawberries sliced, and the cream whipped to save time but don't assemble the dessert until several hours before dinner or it won't hold a good shape. A dessert which looks pretty and also has direct fresh flavours is worth a few minutes' effort.

1½ kg (3 lb) cooking apples, peeled, cored and sliced thinly
¼ tsp ground cinnamon
¾ cup sugar
30 g (1 oz) unsalted butter
1 tbsp orange marmalade
1 punnet (250 g/8 oz) strawberries
2 tbsp red currant jelly
2 tsp brandy
½ cup (4 fl oz) cream

Place the apple into a saucepan with the cinnamon, sugar and butter. Heat gently, stirring once or twice, so the apples become moistened as the butter melts, and won't discolour. Cover the pan and cook gently until quite soft. Purée the apple or, if you like a dish with some texture, you can beat with a wooden spoon to break it up. It needs to be quite stiff so remove the lid and cook over a gentle heat to dry out. Watch and stir because it can caramelise and catch on the base. It should fall from the spoon only with a good firm shake. Add the marmalade and mix through. Cool and refrigerate for at least 12 hours.

Hull the berries and cut each one horizontally into medium to thin slices. Place a poached egg ring, or something similar, onto the individual serving plates. Fill with apple, smoothing the top and pressing down. Lift the egg ring away carefully, and it will leave a nice round base of apple. Arrange the sliced berries on this like the petals of a flower, putting larger centre slices on the outside, and small bits in the centre, leaving a gap. You can overlap them.

Boil the red currant jelly and brandy until syrupy and brush a little on top to glaze. Whip the cream until it holds soft peaks, pipe or spoon a little into the centre to form the heart of the flower. It must be served within a couple of hours or the apple begins to flatten out.

A scatter of crushed toffee in the centre gives the impression of golden stamens.

Serves 6

PRUNES IN A CITRUS TEA SAUCE

The tea flavour in this dessert is not obvious. By the time the prunes are cooked it blends to an elusive fragrant syrup which brings out the taste of the prunes. This dessert keeps beautifully for a week. A word of advice: when you serve this dish, mention to guests that the prunes have been stoned, otherwise I find they discreetly discard the pistachio nuts, assuming they are stones.

2 cups (16 fl oz) china tea
2 tbsp sugar
½ tsp vanilla essence or piece vanilla bean about 2.5 cm (1") in length
2 strips lemon rind
2 strips orange rind
1 tbsp lemon juice
20 dessert prunes
20 pistachio nuts (40 if small)

Heat the china tea with sugar gently. Add vanilla essence or the vanilla bean, split lengthwise down the centre to expose the sticky seeds. Add lemon and orange rind and leave to simmer over low heat for about 5 minutes. Scrape out the seeds from the bean, and return with the outside of the pod to the pot.

Mix in lemon juice and add the prunes. Leave to cook for about 2 minutes, then remove to a bowl and cool. Discard the outside of the vanilla bean and chill the prunes in a covered bowl for 48 hours to allow them to mature in flavour.

Before serving, take the prunes from the liquid and carefully take out the stones without spoiling the shape too much. You can push them back together if they break. Run boiling water over the pistachio nuts and leave to cool until tepid. It should be easy to remove the brown skin. Place a nut inside each prune and arrange the prunes in individual dishes or a larger bowl. Remove the lemon and orange rind strips before pouring the syrup over.

Serves 4

HOT FRUIT DESSERTS

Today, there is such an emphasis on eating fresh fruits and natural foods it is difficult to believe that in medieval times uncooked fruit was regarded with suspicion, and often blamed when a person became ill without apparent reason. Consequently, fruit was cooked for hours until it was soft and pulpy, and 'safe' to eat.

Only some varieties of fruit should be cooked until tender; other fruits, such as strawberries and pineapple, develop acidity when cooked, so should only be warmed through. This is emphasised in the relevant recipes.

Hot fruit desserts are delicious after a cold meal, or on wintry days, and the ingredients of these recipes give flavour to fruits which may be at the end of their season, or less than perfect.

HOT SPICED ORANGES

A simple but very good fast dessert which is refreshing after a rich main meal. It is nicest if you cut the segments from the oranges, so no membrane detracts from the lightness of the fruit. If you find there are not enough segments for each person, use more than four oranges; the number of segments can vary despite outward size or appearance.

The oranges can be cut hours beforehand, refrigerated in a bowl and transfered to the container for baking just before dinner. If juice forms, don't add it to the ovenproof dish when grilling (broiling), or the oranges stew rather than heating quickly. You can keep the juice aside, to drink.

4 large oranges
2 tbsp brown sugar
generous pinch ground cloves
generous pinch ground cinnamon
generous pinch ground allspice
1 tbsp Grand Marnier

Remove the skin and all the white pith from the orange and cut out the segments (so there is no membrane on them). Place into a shallow dish, one in which they will fit in a single layer, if possible.

Mix the sugar with the spices and scatter over the top. Have the griller (broiler) as hot as possible and put the oranges under this until they are heated through.

As they warm, the oranges will become coated with a little juice. Sprinkle the Grand Marnier over the top and serve immediately. This whole procedure should only take about 4–5 minutes.
Serves 4

HOT FRUIT IN A BOOZY SAUCE

The generous portions of alcohol in this dish boil away as the sauce cooks, leaving just the flavour. Delicious on its own, cream detracts and so I think does ice-cream. This is, no doubt, a matter of personal taste. You can't reheat this type of dessert because the sugar in the fruit changes to acid, so it must be cooked just before serving. It is very quick and easy.

Romantic Mangoes (page 15).

Hot Fruit in a Boozy Sauce (page 20)
and Nectarines with a Coconut Topping (page 25).

2 bananas

2 oranges

1 punnet (250 g/8 oz) strawberries

2 kiwi fruit

45 g (1½ oz) butter

1 tbsp sugar

1 tbsp brown sugar

2 tbsp brandy

1 tbsp kirsch

1 tbsp brown rum

Peel the bananas and cut them into thick slices. Peel and remove the pith from the oranges and take out the segments.

Hull the strawberries, and peel and slice the kiwi fruit. (The oranges, strawberries and kiwi fruit can be cut up beforehand and covered with plastic, but the banana must be cut up at the last minute or it will discolour.)

Next, heat the butter in a frying pan, add both sugars and stir until they begin to dissolve. Put the fruit into the pan, toss for about a minute, turning over gently so you don't break it up.

Add the brandy, kirsch and rum and cook until it is bubbling and the fruit is hot. Be careful not to overcook or the fruit will become acid. It takes only a few minutes to cook this dish. Serve immediately.

Serves 4

Autumn Baked Apples

I remember reading that in the French province of Brittany, when the fruit from an orchard was picked, one of the best apples was always left on the highest branch. If it remained until the autumn winds had plucked all the leaves from the trees, farmers believed there would be a good crop the following year.

Simple dishes, like baked apples, often slip from our repertoire as more fashionable desserts appear, yet they are always popular when served, and it is nice to see there is now a trend to serve old-fashioned dishes and puddings — not just for nostalgic reasons but because they often have such uncomplicated and satisfying flavours.

4 cooking apples (such as Granny Smiths)
2 tbsp sultanas, roughly chopped
2 tbsp blanched almonds, roughly chopped
4 dried apricots, cut into strips
rind of 1 small orange
30 g (1 oz) unsalted butter
1 tbsp honey
pinch cinnamon
juice of 1 large orange
4 tsp brown sugar

Peel the apples halfway down, leaving some of the skin on the base, so they will hold a better shape. Remove the cores. Mix the sultanas with the nuts, apricots, orange rind, butter, honey and cinnamon and push this mixture into the apples. Place them in a deep ovenproof casserole dish, one which comes at least level with the top of the fruit.

Add the orange juice. If a large dish, you may need a little more than 1 large orange. Place a teaspoon of brown sugar on top of each apple, like a little cap.

Bake in a moderate oven (180°C/350°F) for about 45 minutes to 1 hour, basting occasionally. The cooking time depends on the type of apple and time of year. If they remain too firm you could place a lid on the dish for 5–10 minutes to soften, but be careful the apples don't fluff and break up. Leave to stand for 5 minutes.

Serve plain or with some running cream. (This dish can be gently reheated as long as the fruit is not overcooked initially.)

Serves 4

Apple and Blackberry Betty

Who was Betty? I can't find a reference to the lady who gave her name to this crumble-topped dessert, always made with sweetened crumbs and butter scattered over apples and baked to a crisp golden brown topping. I'd always imagined an Australian country housewife, a pioneer, immortalising herself by a simple homespun dessert until I came across a recipe for Apple Betty in an American cook book. The important thing is that it is a lovely pudding, enhanced here by the addition of blackberries to give an extra edge of flavour to the apples.

500 g (1 lb) cooking apples (such as Granny Smiths)
¼ cup (2 fl oz) water
¼ cup sugar
grated rind of 1 lemon
250 g (8 oz) blackberries

Peel, core and slice the apples and place into a saucepan with the water, sugar, lemon rind and cover. Cook, giving them an occasional stir until soft. Cool and mix with the blackberries. You can prepare the apple a day before, but it's best not to add the blackberries until the day it is to be cooked or they will become soggy. Place the filling into an ovenproof dish which holds about 5 cups.

TOPPING

½ cup ground almonds
1 cup breadcrumbs (made from stale white or brown bread)
45 g (1½ oz) butter
½ tsp ground cinnamon
¼ cup sugar
2 tbsp chopped blanched almonds

Mix together all the ingredients for the topping and spread evenly over the apples, pressing down gently. Bake in a moderate oven, (180°C/350°F) for about 30 to 35 minutes or until it is lovely and crispy on top and a light brown colour.

Serves 4 (generously)

PEACH CLAFOUTI

Clafouti is a simple rustic dish of fruit with a batter baked so it looks like a tart. As a rule the batter is poured onto the base of the dish, then topped with fruit and another layer of batter over that. This version differs in that the fruit is on the bottom of the dish with a lighter-than-usual clafouti topping. I love it with peaches, the yellow variety. It can, of course, be made with any fruit. It is especially good if made, as it is in Limousin, in France, during cherry season, with a thick layer of fresh pitted dark cherries.

I like it plain, but most of my family like cream over the top.

45 g (1½ oz) unsalted butter
3 medium-sized yellow peaches
2 tbsp sugar

Melt the butter in a frying pan. Peel and slice the peaches and add them, scattering the top with sugar. Cook 3–4 minutes over a fairly high heat, but don't let them break up and occasionally turn or stir gently until softened. Leave to cool.

BATTER

¼ cup flour
½ tsp baking powder
4 eggs
pinch salt
¾ cup (6 fl oz) milk
¼ cup caster sugar
60 g (2 oz) melted butter
icing sugar for dusting the top

To make the batter, whisk or beat all the remaining ingredients together, either in food processor or by hand.

Place the peaches into a shallow ovenproof dish or deep-sided pie dish (20 cm/8″) and pour the batter over the top. It rises as it cooks, so don't fill it to the top. Bake in a moderately hot oven (190°-200°C/375°-400°F) for about 40 minutes or until very puffed and just set when touched in the centre. Shake some icing sugar through a sieve to frost the top, and serve immediately. It subsides very quickly, deflating rather like a soufflé.

Serves 6

Boozy Poached Bananas

Although there seems to be a great quantity of alcohol in this dish, it mellows as it is heated to form a spicy sauce. You can prepare the sauce during the day, adding the bananas about 5 minutes before you want to serve them.

They are nicest of all when they are cooked until a little sloppy but don't look so attractive — this is a dish which tastes rather more splendid than it appears.

¼ cup (2 fl oz) whisky
¼ cup (2 fl oz) brown rum
½ cup (4 fl oz) water
4 tbsp brown sugar
grated rind 1 orange
1 piece cinnamon stick, about 2.5 cm (1") in length
6 medium-sized bananas
1 tbsp thick cream

Choose a frying pan in which the bananas will fit lengthwise. Place the whisky, rum, water, sugar, orange rind and cinnamon stick into this and bring to the boil. Simmer gently, covered with a lid, or use a large plate if you don't have a lid which will fit.

Peel the bananas, cut into halves lengthwise and add, simmering them gently until just soft. (If they are fairly ripe this usually takes about 4 minutes.) Remove the bananas with a long spatula to warmed plates.

Add the cream to the sauce, bring to the boil, mixing until it heats. Pour the sauce over the bananas, distributing as evenly as possible. Discard the cinnamon stick, and serve.

Serves 6

Nectarines with a Coconut Topping

The fruit for this should be firm, but not rock hard, and green or it takes too long to cook and lacks flavour. The slight sharpness of the stoned fruit is in wonderful contrast to the crunchiness of coconut and blanched almonds as they become slightly toasted and nutty.

Easy to prepare, but nice enough for any occasion, served on some green leaves with a tiny bowl of either vanilla ice-cream or plain cream alongside.

6 firm nectarines
½ cup desiccated coconut
¼ cup sugar
2 tbsp blanched almonds, finely chopped
1 tsp ground cinnamon
45 g (1½ oz) butter

Wash the nectarines, but don't peel them, and cut each one into halves. Remove the stones and a little of the flesh from the centre cavity. If you take out the red section (around the stone) this will leave a large enough space for filling.

Mix the coconut with sugar, almonds and cinnamon. Cut the butter into small pieces and rub through the coconut mixture with your fingertips. The filling will look dry but, once it warms and the butter melts, will be very moist.

Spoon into the fruit and place in a shallow dish so they fit with just a little space between. Add a couple of tablespoons of water to the dish to give moisture.

Bake in a moderate oven (180°C/350°F) until the fruit is tender and the topping a light brown on top. About 25 minutes is usually enough time, but judge by the look and feel, rather than the timing.

Serves 6

Cherry gratin

This dish is a harmony of deep crimson and cream, with little curves of cherry rising to bob through the topping.

You need individual gratin dishes because this dessert doesn't look attractive served at the table from a large container, and it is difficult to spoon out even amounts of cherries, topping and juices.

Serve it on its own. Cream and ice-cream are quite unnecessary.

500 g (1 lb) stoned cherries
½ cup (4 fl oz) red wine
2 tbsp red currant jelly
a piece of cinnamon stick, about 2.5 cm (1") in length
3 egg yolks
2 tbsp brown sugar
½ cup (4 fl oz) cream
1 tbsp brandy
a little cinnamon

Cook the cherries gently with the wine, red currant jelly and cinnamon stick in a covered pan for about 5 minutes. They should be tender, but not too soft. Leave them to cool and refrigerate. If you can do this part of the dish the day before the flavour will improve through standing. The leftover liquid is not used in the dish, but you could serve it as a sauce alongside, or freeze and keep for preparing some stewed cherries another time.

Divide the cherries into 4 gratin dishes.

Beat the yolks with the sugar and cream, adding the brandy last. Pour over the top of each dish — there won't be quite enough mixture to cover the cherries.

Scatter the top with a little cinnamon, not too much or it will be too dominating.

Bake in a moderate oven (180°C/350°F) for about 15–18 minutes. The mixture should be set on the edges, but you have to leave it a little soft in the centre so it tastes creamy. As it stands it sets more so it's best to leave 5 minutes before taking to the table. Serve warm, rather than bubbling hot.

Serves 4

Coconut Bananas in a Citrus Sauce

A good dessert to remember when you don't have much time. The lemon and orange sharpen the blandness of cooked banana. Nice by itself or with vanilla ice-cream.

4 firm but slightly ripe bananas
30 g unsalted butter, melted
2 tbsp brown sugar
½ tsp ground cinnamon
⅓ cup (2½ oz) orange juice
1 tbsp lemon juice
3 tbsp desiccated coconut

Peel the bananas and cut them into halves lengthwise. Place in an ovenproof dish. Pour the butter over the top and scatter on brown sugar, cinnamon and orange and lemon juice. Bake (uncovered) in a moderate oven for about 10–12 minutes, or until soft. No need to turn them, but if the sauce is reducing too much and the bananas are still firm it is best to cover the dish at this stage.

While the bananas are cooking, toast the coconut in a dry frying pan, stirring frequently so it will colour evenly.

Arrange several pieces of banana on each plate, then spoon the sauce on top. Sprinkle coconut over them.

Serves 4

Blackberry and Nectarine Crunch

This crumble mixture is superior to many — some toppings are too heavy with flour — and could be used to top other fruits, such as apple, apricot or peaches.

The blackberries stain the nectarines with a deep purple colour as they give out juices, and the combination is really very good.

250 g (8 oz) firm, but not too green, nectarines
250 g (8 oz) blackberries
½ cup sugar
1 tbsp cornflour (cornstarch)

Wash but don't peel the nectarines, and cut them into slices. Put into a bowl with the blackberries and scatter sugar and cornflour on top. Stir so it coats the fruit. Put into an ovenproof dish that holds about 4 cups of mixture.

TOPPING

½ cup hazelnuts, roughly chopped
2 tbsp flour
90 g (3 oz) butter
⅓ cup brown sugar
¼ tsp ground cinnamon
¾ cup breadcrumbs, made from stale white or brown bread
¼ cup desiccated coconut

For the topping, mix the nuts and flour together in a bowl with all the remaining dry ingredients. Melt the butter and add, stirring so it is well-blended. It will be quite moist. Spread the topping over the fruit, as evenly as possible.

Bake in a moderate oven (180°C/350°F) for about 30 minutes, or until it is juicy and bubbling at the edges and the top is crunchy and light brown in colour. Let settle for at least 5 minutes before serving; it is best if eaten warm rather than very hot.

For reheating, place in a moderate oven for about 10 to 12 minutes.

Serves 6

PINEAPPLE BAKED IN SWEET ORANGE BUTTER

Buy baby pineapples for this if you can, so you can serve half to each person. If you can't, use a large pineapple and spoon the fruit out of the shell into dishes at the table. It is most important not to overcook pineapple. When you grill the top, have the heat high and preheated so the buttery mixture will melt and glaze quickly. Pineapple tastes quite acid instead of sweet, if cooked too long.

3 baby pineapples
90 g (3 oz) unsalted butter
3 tbsp icing sugar
3 tbsp brown sugar
grated rind 1 large orange
2 tbsp white rum

Cut the pineapples in halves lengthwise, slicing as evenly as you can through the green tops so they both have a similar section of green. Remove the flesh from the shell. This is easiest if you have a curved grapefruit knife; if not, a small sharp knife held on a tilt will do the job. Cut the flesh into neat dice, any scrappy pieces can be put underneath. If doing this hours beforehand, leave the pineapple flesh out of the shells or they become wet, and turn the shells cut side down on a bench or board so they remain fresh as the juice drains away.

Cream all the ingredients for the butter (except the white rum) in a food processor, or by hand.

When ready to cook fill the shells with the pineapple pieces and dot the top with little bits of the butter. Place under the grill, with the green top extending outside so it won't burn, until the butter is just bubbling.

Warm the rum in a small pot and ignite. Pour a little over the top of each pineapple half and serve immediately.

Serves 6

BAKED APPLE SLICES WITH WHISKY SULTANAS

This is not the most attractive-looking dessert. It has a plain homely look, but the aroma is wonderful and it tastes more exciting than it looks. Very good with thick cream.

2 tbsp sultanas (golden raisins)
2 tbsp whisky, bourbon or brown rum
500 g (1 lb) cooking apples
½ cup (4 fl oz) apricot jam
1 tbsp brown sugar
¼ cup (2 fl oz) water
2 tbsp lemon juice
an additional tbsp whisky, bourbon or brown rum (optional)

Place the sultanas into a bowl and pour the whisky, bourbon or rum over the top. Leave to stand for about an hour, but it doesn't hurt if you leave them all day. Most of the alcohol will be absorbed.

Peel, core and slice the apples and put them into an ovenproof dish with a 4-cup capacity.

Warm the apricot jam with brown sugar, water, lemon juice and, when bubbling on the edges and the sugar and jam are blended, pour over the apples. Add the sultanas and, if there is any whisky left in the bowl, pour this over too and stir so the apples are well-coated with the liquid.

Place in a moderate oven (180°C/350°F) and bake until the apples are tender, giving them a stir once or twice. Cooking time depends very much on which variety of apple you use. Granny Smith apples, for example, take about 30 minutes. Don't cover the dish or the apples may fluff and lose their shape. When they are ready, warm the whisky, bourbon or rum and ignite. Pour over the apples and leave to burn away. This will freshen the flavour.

Serve the dish hot or warm. It can be reheated if you wish; about 15 minutes (covered) in a moderate oven, should be enough.
Serves 4

Apple and Strawberry Strudel

I first tasted this version of strudel on a paddle steamer, the *Emmy Lou*, as it travelled slowly down the Murray River. We'd all eaten a casual cold picnic lunch, and the strudel came on a long platter, the layered thin sheets sugary and nutty and scented with butter and apples, and the slight acidity of the cooked strawberry surprisingly good.

The canned apples made for pies, usually unsweetened, are very successful in strudel. If you prefer to cook your own, be sure they are well-drained or the crust will become soggy. I have made this dessert with filo pastry layered with butter, mostly used as a home alternative to the true strudel dough, which requires skill, practice and patience to pull out to an almost transparent sheet without breaking into holes.

I find this dish doesn't reheat well — the strawberries become too soft and acid — but it can be prepared several hours before baking.

½ cup finely chopped walnuts
⅓ cup fine white breadcrumbs
¼ cup caster sugar
200 g (6½ oz) can of pie-pack apples, unsweetened or 1½ cups cooked apple, well-drained
125 g (4 oz) whole small strawberries
2 tbsp roughly chopped walnuts
6 sheets filo pastry
unsalted butter
icing sugar (confectioner's sugar)

Mix the finely chopped walnuts, crumbs and sugar together. Add the strawberries and roughly chopped nuts to the apple and mix together gently.

Melt about 60 g (2 oz) butter in a saucepan. You may need more but it is better to melt small quantities at a time.

Place one sheet of filo on a bench, butter lightly and scatter with a few of the nuts and crumbs. Place another layer of filo on top of this, butter lightly, then add more nuts and crumbs, continuing until you have six layers, reserving a spoonful of the mixture for placing under the apple. Scatter this on, then top with apples and strawberries.

Make a long shape, leaving sufficient filo at both ends to fold under. Roll over to enclose and tuck the ends under. Carefully lift and place on a lightly-buttered flat baking tray. Brush the top with a little more butter. Be sparing or it will be too rich. Bake in a moderately hot oven (200°C/400°F) until crisp and golden. It usually takes about 25 minutes. Sieve some icing sugar over the top and serve warm.

Serves 8

ICE-CREAMS

Ice-cream, once regarded as an easy, everyday dessert coming in a few creamy but conventional flavours, was lifted to an elaborate culinary presentation by three star French chefs, the Trois Gros brothers. They named their creation 'The Grand Dessert'. A platter of sorbets and ice-cream with fresh and velvety-smooth flavours, varying as the seasons went by, were arranged with dainty portions of fruit and spoonfuls of light sauce.

This style of dessert, in a less complicated form, has remained very popular in restaurants. It is easy to make in a simpler style at home. One of the reasons this is possible is the number of ice-cream machines on the market which churn the mixture to a creamy, professional smoothness.

If you don't have a machine, instructions are given here as to how to achieve the best and smoothest texture. But you must follow ice-cream recipes carefully. The sugar measurement is most important: too much and the ice-cream or sorbet will not set properly. High alcohol has the same result. If, however, you add too little sugar, the texture will be grainy, sometimes with tiny fragments of ice throughout.

The temperatures of freezers in different brands of home refrigerators can vary a little. If you make an ice-cream which is not perfect the first time, you can adjust the recipes yourself by adding a little more, or perhaps less sugar.

It is only worth making fruit ice-creams when the fruit is in season, ripe and the most perfect you can buy. Poor or damaged fruit makes an equally poor ice-cream.

VANILLA ICE-CREAM

Made by a classic method, this is a rich custard which has been flavoured with the sweet, rounded flavour of the vanilla bean. It will, of course, have small dark specks from the bean: an indication of true vanilla creams. If you don't want to use a vanilla bean, flavour after the custard is made with ½–1 teaspoon of vanilla essence, the amount depends on the strength of flavouring required.

½ vanilla bean
*1 cup (8 fl oz) milk**
1 cup (8 fl oz) cream
6 egg yolks
¾ cup caster sugar

**For an even richer ice-cream, substitute a second cup of cream for the cup of milk.*

Split the vanilla bean lengthwise to expose the inside soft section. Put into a saucepan with the milk and cream and heat gently until the liquid is almost boiling. Remove from the heat and leave to steep for about 10 minutes.

Beat the yolks with sugar until thick and pale. Gradually add the milk and cream to the yolks, stirring as you do so, and return to the saucepan. Cook the mixture, stirring constantly with a wooden spoon or using a whisk. When it is a light custard, remove. Don't let it boil. Stir for a few minutes, because it will continue cooking on the base.

Remove the bean and scrape the moist inside from the centre into the custard. Cool and then churn the mixture or freeze in the refrigerator.

Serves 4–6

CHERRY ICE-CREAM

I have rarely seen a cherry ice-cream on a restaurant menu, or been served one, perhaps because this precious fruit is in for such a short season, gone from the shops before we become tired of it. Use deep red or black sweet cherries, the best flavoured ones you can buy, and the ice-cream will reward you with an intensity of colour and all the depth of the fruit in its flavour.

500 g (1 lb) ripe, sweet cherries
¼ cup (2 fl oz) water
1 tbsp sugar
2 strips orange rind
1 tsp red currant jelly
1¼ cups (10 fl oz) cream
3 egg yolks
⅔ cup sugar
½ tsp vanilla essence

Stone the cherries. This is both time-consuming and a nuisance, but you have no choice when making an ice-cream. Place them into a saucepan with the water, sugar and orange rind and cook very gently until tender. Add the red currant jelly and stir. Purée the mixture, the juices as well as the fruit. You should have 1¼ cups of cherry pulp. Leave to cool.

Heat the cream for the custard; and while it is warming beat the yolks and sugar until thick and pale. Gradually add the hot cream, whisking all the time, and return to the saucepan. Whisk until it is lightly thickened — don't let the custard boil — and remove from the heat to a bowl as soon as ready. Flavour with vanilla. Cool and mix with the cherry pulp.

Freeze in an ice-cream machine or in a tray in the refrigerator.

Serves 6

STRAWBERRY ICE-CREAM

One of my favourite berry ice-creams, there is no custard to alter the flavour; just berries, sugar and cream. It is easy to make and intensely strawberry-flavoured. But don't bother to make it unless strawberries are in season, fragrant and sun-ripe.

250 g (8 oz) ripe strawberries
¾ cup caster sugar
3 tsp lemon juice
1 cup (8 fl oz) very thick cream

Hull the berries and chop them into halves. Process in a food processor until you have a purée. Don't leave any large pieces of fruit or they become icy. A few tiny bits will give some texture. Or you can put the strawberries through a sieve, then mash a few separately to give the same texture. Mix the sugar into the berries and stir well, leave to stand a few minutes, to soften. Add lemon juice.

Whisk or whip the cream until it holds soft peaks. Add the strawberry pulp and stir to mix thoroughly. Freeze in an ice-cream machine according to the manufacturer's directions or in a tray in the refrigerator.

Serves 4

PEACH ICE-CREAM

Quite a wonderful peach-flavoured ice-cream, it is adapted from a recipe in *Chez Panisse Desserts*.

1¼ cups (10 fl oz) cream
3 egg yolks
¾ cup sugar
500 g (1 lb) ripe yellow peaches
1 tbsp lemon juice
additional tbsp sugar

Heat the cream until almost boiling. While it is warming, beat the egg yolks and sugar until thick and pale. Add the cream gradually, whisking or stirring and return to the heat. Cook, stirring or whisking constantly, until a lightly thickened custard. Be careful not to let the mixture come to the boil. Put into a basin and leave aside until quite cold, stirring occasionally.

Once it is cool, peel and slice the peaches. Scatter lemon juice and sugar over the top, stir so the peaches are coated, and leave them standing for about an hour. Take out about a quarter of the peach and purée the remainder in a food processor or a moulin. Mash the portion of sliced peaches you retained until in tiny bits. A potato masher is good for this or you can use a fork, first putting the peaches on a flat dinner plate.

Mix the peach purée and mashed peaches into the custard and churn in an ice-cream machine, according to the manufacturer's directions, or freeze in a tray. When frozen on the edges, beat again until creamy, and refreeze.

Serve on its own or with some fresh peach slices.

Serves 4 generously

PASSIONFRUIT ICE-CREAM

The intense flavour of this fruit comes through even when frozen, but you will need a lot of pulp. There would be far too many black pips if you added all the passionfruit without sieving. A few crunchy seeds are enough to give texture to the golden, creamy mixture.

¾ cup (6 fl oz) milk
¾ cup (6 fl oz) cream
6 egg yolks
1 cup caster sugar
8 passionfruit, or 10 if small

Heat the milk and cream together in a saucepan. While they are warming beat the yolks with sugar until thick and pale in colour. Gradually add the hot milk and cream, whisking or stirring constantly. Return to the saucepan and cook, stirring constantly with a whisk until the mixture has lightly thickened. Don't let it boil. Lift the saucepan off the heat, if cooking on the base. Tip into a basin and leave to cool, stirring occasionally.

Cut the passionfruit into halves, lengthwise so it is easier to fill the ice-cream back into the shells for serving. Add the pulp and seeds of 4 passionfruit. Place the remaining 4 passionfruit into a sieve and press down to get out as much juice as possible. Don't add *all* the whole passionfruit or the ice-cream will be too pippy. Altogether you need about ½ cup (4 fl oz) of seeds and pulp. Mix well and churn in an ice-cream machine, according to the manufacturer's directions; or freeze in a tray, and beat again when solid on the edges.

Put the solid ice-cream back into the passionfruit shells, smoothing to the top as evenly as possible. Store in the freezer, covering each one with plastic wrap.

Serve on some of the glossy passionfruit leaves, if you have a vine, or small grape leaves. Sometimes I find I have more ice-cream than needed for this number of shells; it depends on their size. You may need to buy a couple of extra passionfruit if you want to use up all the ice-cream.

Serves 4–6

Light Orange and Walnut Pudding (page 93).

A summer Christmas treat: Chocolate and Fruit Layered Ice-cream (page 40).

EXTRA RICH CHOCOLATE ICE-CREAM WITH COGNAC-SOAKED SULTANAS

Serve small portions: not only is it very rich, but it's also rather dense in texture. It is enormously popular.

2 tbsp sultanas (golden raisins)
2 tbsp cognac
¼ cup brown sugar
¼ cup (2 fl oz) water
½ cup (4 fl oz) cream
90 g (3 oz) dark sweetened chocolate
additional ½ cup (4 fl oz) cream
½ cup (4 fl oz) milk

Put the sultanas into a bowl and add the cognac. Leave to stand for 12 hours, longer if you wish. (They should absorb all the alcohol.) Put the sugar and water into a saucepan, and warm gently until the sugar has dissolved. Don't stir, but you can give the pan an occasional shake. Turn up the heat and cook until it is a dark golden caramel. Add the cream and return to the heat so any hard bits of toffee will melt. Cool slightly.

Break the chocolate into squares and add to the warm caramel cream. Leave aside; there should be enough heat to melt the chocolate. Give it a stir once or twice. If there are any firm bits of chocolate you can return the pan for a few minutes to melt, but don't warm too much. Leave aside to cool and mix in the cream and milk, stirring well.

Put into an ice-cream machine and churn, according to the manufacturer's directions. Add the sultanas 5 minutes before it is firm, and churn again.

If you're not using an ice-cream machine, mix the sultanas through when you put the mixture into metal trays in the freezer, stirring once or twice or the fruit may sink to the base. There is no need to whip this ice-cream again if you freeze in the tray. It is very rich and never becomes icy.

Serves 4

Ginger and Macadamia Nut Ice-Cream

The Hawaiian macadamia nut dominated the market for years, yet the trees originally came from Australia. Macadamia nuts are now being processed in large quantities in Australia. Despite this, the macadamia is still an expensive nut. However, the flavour is unique. Toasted, they have even more flavour. When you cut them for recipes such as in this cake, chop by hand; processors will chop them unevenly, and the fine bits burn easily in the oven. If you can't get any ginger in syrup (which comes in those pretty Chinese jars) use crystallised ginger, washing away the sugar coating. The ginger syrup can be omitted, but don't try to substitute anything else and never use powdered ginger. It is horrible in ice-cream.

90 g (3 oz) unsalted macadamia nuts
1 cup (8 fl oz) milk
1 cup (8 fl oz) cream
6 egg yolks
¾ cup caster sugar
¼ tsp vanilla essence
2 tbsp finely diced glacé ginger
1 tbsp ginger syrup from a jar

Chop the macadamia nuts fairly finely by hand. Toast them by placing on a tray in the oven or cook in a dry frying pan, stirring almost constantly until evenly coloured. Leave to cool.

Warm the milk and cream together until almost boiling. While they are heating, beat the yolks with caster sugar until thick and pale. Gradually add the milk and cream to the yolks, stirring constantly, and return to the saucepan. Cook, stirring with a whisk, until a light custard. Don't let it boil.

Remove to a bowl and add the vanilla essence, ginger and ginger syrup. Leave to cool completely, then stir in the nuts and freeze in an ice-cream machine or in the freezer.

ESPRESSO TORTONI

A tortoni is an iced confection rather than an ice-cream. It is easy to make and quite delicious. The armaretti which flavour this are the crisp little Italian macaroons usually sold in packets. They are sweet, yet sharp with the taste of bitter almonds.

4 tbsp caster sugar

¼ cup (2 fl oz) strong coffee

2 tbsp brandy

1 cup (8 fl oz) cream

½ cup crushed almond macaroons (armaretti)

1 egg white

2 tbsp grated dark sweet chocolate

Mix the caster sugar with coffee and brandy.

Whip the cream until it holds soft peaks. Add the coffee mixture and almond macaroons.

Beat the egg white until stiff, but don't overbeat, and fold through about a third at a time.

Spoon into small coffee cups or individual dishes and freeze.

This mixture is not one which is churned in an ice-cream machine. It freezes beautifully without needing to be beaten. Before serving, scatter the top with a little grated chocolate or some chocolate curls.

This frozen dessert is best eaten within 36 hours.

Serves 6

Chocolate and Fruit Layered Ice-Cream

A fruity chocolate pudding that you could serve at Christmas time or for dinner parties. Very creamy and smooth, it's not too complicated, as you don't have to make a custard base.

4 eggs
2 cups (16 fl oz) cream
⅓ cup sugar
2 tbsp kirsch
100 g (3 ¼ oz) dark sweet chocolate
1 cup finely diced mixed glacé fruit

Break the chocolate into squares and put into a bowl. Stand this over a saucepan of simmering water and leave to melt. Pour the kirsch over the fruit and leave to marinate while mixing the ice-cream.

Separate the eggs. Whip the whites until stiff. Whip the cream until it holds very soft peaks, and fold the whites and cream together.

Beat the yolks with the sugar until thick and pale and mix into the cream and egg white mixture. Divide into halves and put into two bowls.

Add the glacé fruit to one bowl. Into the other, mix the chocolate, stir well and then return this to the larger portion of mixture.

Use a bowl or container which can be put in the freezer: a steam pudding basin, or a smooth domed copper mould can be used. It should hold about 5 cups.

Place a thin layer of chocolate filling on the base. On top of this place a layer of the fruit filling, then the chocolate filling, and so on, continuing until you have used up all the mixture. The layers will not be exactly even. It doesn't matter if they are even a little marbled; this gives a more natural effect than if machine-perfect.

Freeze. It takes about 6 hours to firm as a rule, although this depends on the freezer.

This is not an ice-cream mixture which can be kept too long as the sugar in the glacé fruit will begin to soften it after a couple of days. Dip into warm water to loosen and turn out onto a serving plate. You can decorate the base with a little whipped cream to neaten before serving, if you wish.

As a Christmas dessert, this can be decorated by pouring a mixture of chocolate and cream over the top. Heat ¼ cup of cream. Add 45 g of grated dark chocolate and leave to melt. Stir and trickle over the top. Freeze.

Serves 8

ORANGE SORBET

A spoonful of lemon freshens the orange in this refreshing dessert. Ideal to serve after rich food, it can be made in advance. It's a help if you have an ice-cream machine; you'll get a finer texture.

Top chefs say to make sorbets at the last moment, but this is not really an ideal situation for the home cook. I do think sorbets are best eaten on the day they are made. If you rely on a freezer rather than a machine, freeze it until set around the edges, leaving it soft in the centre. Tip the mixture into a bowl and beat at high speed until smooth. Return and freeze. It can be scooped into oval shapes with a dessertspoon for serving or filled into small orange, or lemon halves which have had all the pulp removed. Heap a few shiny shreds of glacé orange peel on top for a pretty effect.

1 cup (8 fl oz) water

2 cups sugar

grated rind 1 large or 2 small oranges

2 cups (16 fl oz) orange juice

1 tbsp lemon juice

Put the water and sugar into a saucepan and warm gently, shaking occasionally until the sugar has dissolved.

Add the orange rind and cook until the mixture is a thick syrup. Now add the orange juice and lemon juice and leave to cool completely.

Churn in an ice-cream machine according to the manufacturer's directions or freeze in the refrigerator. If doing the latter, remove when icy and beat again, then return to the freezer.

Serves 4

Creams, Custards and Sauces

A simple bowl of fresh fruits, when perfectly ripe, can be served absolutely plain. If you want to glamorise it you can serve with one of these flavoured creams, being careful that they add to the dish and don't conflict in any way. Full of bubbles from a glass of champagne, refreshing with yoghurt or tart with lemon, these creams give a finish not only to fruits but to plainly-flavoured puddings.

Cream is a luxury, a gilding of the lily perhaps, but desserts and cream seem to go together, like 'buttercups and daisies', in the words of English writer Margaret Costa.

A variety of creams are sold on the market: reduced with some of the butterfat removed, thick and suitable for whipping, and pure cream with a very high butterfat content. This last one is usually so thick that it should be served plain on the table, and is not always suitable for whipping. Reduced cream will mostly be too light for piping but can be poured over desserts. Thickened cream can be used for pouring or whipping. Be careful never to overbeat any cream. When you are piping it can become buttery with the warmth of your hand as you hold the piping bag. Whisk cream only until it maintains a shape.

Lemon cream

Refreshing and slightly tart, this goes well with any of the berry fruits: strawberries, loganberries, mulberries, youngberries and blueberries. The exception is the raspberry. These fragile berries are really nicest with plain running cream or chantilly cream.

½ cup (4 fl oz) sour cream
½ tsp grated lemon rind
1 tbsp lemon juice
2 tbsp icing sugar
generous pinch cinnamon
½ tsp vanilla essence

If the sour cream is very thin, whisk it a little first, so it holds a light shape. Add the lemon rind, juice and sugar and flavour with cinnamon and vanilla.

Chill for several hours so the flavours blend. It can be stored for several days. The longer it is kept, the more it will thicken.

Chantilly cream

A glamorous name for whipped, slightly sweetened cream. There are no tricks except it is important the cream is very cold and whipped only until it holds peaks. An extra beat or two and it loses its smooth texture, and can become slightly buttery.

1 cup (8 fl oz) very cold cream
few drops vanilla essence
2 tbsp icing sugar (confectioner's sugar)

Whip the cream slightly, add the icing sugar and vanilla essence and continue whipping until soft peaks form. You can use an electric beater but be cautious as it thickens quickly. A whisk is slower but gives a lovely texture.

Keep the cream chilled and cover so it doesn't pick up any taste from other foods stored in the refrigerator.

Champagne cream

Don't make the mistake of thinking a glass of white wine will do just as well as champagne. Champagne is generally less acid than white wine and, most importantly, gives a slight spritzig taste on the tongue: an effect of bubbles which is refreshing and interesting.

A lovely cream with berry fruits, or any fruits that can take a slightly sharper-flavoured cream than the plain variety. The rest of the champagne bottle can be sipped with the dessert or, if it doesn't go well, afterwards as a palate cleanser. If there is any left over, you can recork it for a short time and store in the refrigerator. The bottle will retain its bubbles and sparkle for a day, the better the quality of the champagne, the longer it lasts.

2/3 cup champagne
3 tbsp caster sugar
1 cup cream
additional 3 tbsp champagne

Mix the champagne with sugar and leave to stand until the sugar has softened.

Whip the cream until it holds firm peaks and gently stir or whisk in the champagne and sugar. It will be a soft, lightly textured cream. Chill for several hours.

Just before serving add the remaining champagne. It will make the cream fizz slightly. Serve immediately — while still bubbling.

Yoghurt cream

The slight sharpness of yoghurt cuts the richness of plain cream. It is mixed with coconut, although you can omit this if you prefer a smooth texture, and sweetened with vanilla and apricot jam. Serve alongside fresh fruits, apricots or peaches.

½ cup (4 fl oz) natural yoghurt
½ cup (4 fl oz) lightly whipped cream
2 tbsp desiccated coconut
½ tsp vanilla essence
2 tbsp apricot jam

Stir the yoghurt and cream together. Then add the coconut and vanilla essence.

Push the apricot jam through a sieve. Sometimes it is easier to do this if you warm the jam first. You will lose some of the quantity in the sieve, but the cream should still be quite sweet enough. Taste and, if not right for your needs, add a little more jam.

Chill for at least several hours.

It keeps well for a couple of days, covered in the refrigerator.

Serves 6–8 as an accompaniment for fruits

SAYBAYON

A frothy airy mixture of eggs and wine, usually served warm with plain vanilla puddings or berry fruits. An impractical sauce for most cooks, requiring as it does lots of last-minute whipping over heat. It is easier for a chef who is concentrating only on cooking and not on being host or hostess at the same time.

This chilled version can be prepared in advance. The added cream helps to stabilise the saybayon, which can separate as it cools. Don't keep too long. It loses volume, so eat within 8 hours.

3 egg yolks

4 tbsp sugar

¼ cup (2 fl oz) dry white wine

1 tbsp Grand Marnier

¼ cup (2 fl oz) cream

Place the egg yolks into a bowl which will fit over a saucepan or into the top of a double boiler. Add the sugar, white wine and Grand Marnier. Beat over simmering water. It will double and become very frothy. When well risen the mixture should hold a peak; remove and continue beating for a minute. Leave to become cool.

Whip the cream until stiff and fold gently into the frothy egg, then chill.

Serves 6

Egg custard

One of the classic sauces — usually called Crème Anglaise — which is simple to make. Just be careful never to let it boil, and stir constantly so it is smooth and creamy. If you make a mistake, and the mixture bubbles on the edges, add a tablespoon of cold milk or cream and whisk like fury to lower the temperature, removing it instantly from the heat. An uneven sauce can be sieved or put into a blender to save it, although the texture will never be as good.

Egg custard is usually made with vanilla flavouring, preferably a vanilla pod which gives a rounder taste and perfume. A tablespoon of brandy, cognac, orange liqueur or some other flavoured liqueur (whatever you think will blend suitably with the dessert this sauce is to accompany) can also be used to ring changes in the flavouring.

½ vanilla bean, split into halves
¾ cup (6 fl oz) cream
½ cup (4 fl oz) milk
2 tbsp caster sugar
6 egg yolks

Heat the cream with the milk and vanilla bean until almost boiling. Remove from the heat and leave to cool. When ready to make the sauce, heat this mixture again. (You can skip this step if you are using vanilla essence.)

Whisk the sugar and egg yolks until they are pale and thick. Pour the hot cream and milk into the bowl, stirring or whisking constantly.

Combine well and return the mixture to the saucepan. Cook, stirring all the time with a spoon, or a whisk until it lightly coats the back of the spoon. Be very careful not to let it boil.

Take off the heat and remove the vanilla bean. Scrape out the sticky centre and return this to the custard. Pour through a sieve into a bowl. Stir occasionally until cold and chill for several hours.

It can be kept several days in the refrigerator, covered, and will thicken more when chilled. If you don't want to use vanilla bean, flavour with about half a teaspoon of vanilla essence when the custard is cooked.

Serves 6

Brandy sauce

Brandy was always used in copious quantities in sauces to accompany English plum puddings. One of the reasons is that brandy was cheap, costing less than a cup of coffee or tea.

1½ cups (12 fl oz) milk
1 tbsp sugar
2 tsp cornflour (cornstarch)
1 tbsp water
1 large egg
¼ cup (2 fl oz) brandy

Warm the milk and sugar until beginning to bubble on the edges. Mix the cornflour with water to make a paste and add a few spoonfuls of the warm milk to this, then return to the heat and cook until boiling and lightly thickened.

Whisk the egg with the brandy in a bowl, and gradually tip in the hot milk, stirring constantly. Return this to the pan but be careful not to let the sauce boil once you have added the egg, or it will curdle.

If you need to keep this sauce warm, put it in a double boiler or stand the saucepan in a frying pan with hot water around.

PIES AND TARTS

It was the Romans who first had the idea of sealing a filling, usually meat or fish, inside a paste made of oil and flour to cook it. When the filling was ready the case was cracked open, the inside eaten, and the outside discarded.

These first 'pies' were later made with a mixture more like our pastry — with butter and flour — and the fillings gradually became richer: not just fruit but chocolate, creams and custards, chestnuts and even flowers were used to give an enormous variety.

A pie or tart is a dish best served after a light main course, or perhaps when the rest of the meal has been cold and you want to finish with something warming and substantial. The pastry you use is very important. It's no good cheating or skimping on this; casings must be fine, buttery and light. A food processor takes most of the tedious work out of preparing pastry, giving a batch in a couple of minutes.

I never use a floured board to roll my pastry. It can spoil the proportions of the mixture. Instead, I roll it between waxed paper. Put a sheet of paper on your bench, place the flattened round piece of pastry on top, then over this put another piece of waxed paper. Roll out, but only once. You must then loosen the paper or it will stick to the pastry. Simply lift up (and replace) the paper on top and then turn the whole lot over and repeat this procedure with the paper which was underneath. Roll again and repeat, lifting the paper each time until the pastry is the right size and shape. It only takes a couple of minutes and, even on a hot day, you will find buttery pastries manageable.

Remove the top sheet, invert your pastry into a pie plate or dish, gently peel away the second sheet, and trim the edges of the pastry.

If the recipe says to bake first, before adding the filling, be sure to do this. There's nothing worse than soggy pastry on the base of a pie.

NECTARINE AND PEACH TART

Nectarines are sharper, yet richer than peaches, which have a soft, velvety sweetness. Combined in a tart, each seems to emphasise the best features of the other. Nectarines, like peaches, can be white or yellow. For this dish, use the yellow variety of both. There is always a slight gamble buying stoned fruits: the most perfect appearance and large size, at a high price, do not always denote flavour. Sometimes it is best to buy small fruit. Choose ripe rather than hard ones, so the flavour is sweet and full rather than tart.

HOT WATER CRUST

[Makes enough for a double crust in a 20 cm (8") pie dish]

90 g (3 oz) butter
3 tbsp boiling water
1 cup flour
½ cup self-raising flour
pinch salt

Cut the butter into small pieces. This pastry is most easily made in a food processor, but you can use an electric mixer or beater. You can mix it by hand but this will take much longer. Add the boiling water and process or beat until creamy.

Sift both types of flour with salt and again process or mix until it forms a paste.

Wrap in some greaseproof paper and leave to rest for 30 minutes in a cool place in the kitchen. If it is too sticky you can scatter a little flour on the pastry as you roll, but be careful not to add too much or it will taste of uncooked flour on the outside. It is a slightly sticky mixture but, if rolled between some greaseproof or waxed greaseproof paper, it is easy to handle.

Cut it into portions of ⅓ and ⅔, and role out the larger piece for the base. Fit into the pie tin, taking it to the top edge.

Put the nectarine and peach filling into the base.

Roll out the second, smaller, portion of pastry and place on top. Cut, leaving it a little larger than the top of the pie dish. Pinch together with the bottom portion of pastry along the edges. Cut two or three slits in the top.

Brush the pastry with cream and scatter lightly with sugar to give a crunchy top. Bake in a moderate oven (180°C/350°F) for about 35–40 minutes, until the pastry is light brown and firm to touch. Leave to rest for 10 minutes before slicing, so the juices will settle.

FILLING

3 ripe peaches (about 375 g/12 oz)
3 ripe nectarines (about 375 g/12 oz)
¼ cup sugar
¼ cup brown sugar
½ tsp ground cinnamon
1 tsp grated orange rind
2 tbsp flour

Cut the peaches into slices. You can skin them first if you wish. There's no need to skin the nectarines, which should be cut into similar-sized slices to the peaches.

Place the fruit into a bowl and scatter the remaining ingredients over the top. Toss so the the fruit is coated.

Serves 8

OLD-FASHIONED APPLE PIE

Of all the delicates that Britons try,
To please the palate and delight the eye
Of all the sev'ral kinds of sumptuous fare
There is none that can with apple pie compare.

William King (1663-1712)

Despite elaborate and fashionable new desserts, apple pie still remains a favourite. A warm, comforting type of dish, apple slices are mixed with sugar and lemon and cooked to a soft slightly tart pulp inside a light buttery crust.

Use a cooking apple for this version. I like Granny Smith — the variety that put Australia on the apple map — thanks to Maria (Granny) Smith who grew the first tree outside her back door.

1 quantity of pastry (see previous recipe)
1 kg (2 lb) cooking apples, such as Granny Smith
½ tsp cinnamon
pinch cloves
5 tbsp sugar
grated rind ½ lemon
2 tsp lemon juice
milk (for brushing on pastry)
some caster sugar to frost the pie

Divide the pastry into two pieces, one slightly larger for the base. Butter a pie dish, 20 cm (8″) in size, and line the base with rolled out pastry.

Peel and core the apples and place in a bowl. Scatter the cinnamon, cloves, sugar, lemon rind and juice over the top, and toss until mixed throughout. Heap the apples in the pie shell, doming them slightly in the centre.

Lay the second portion of rolled pastry over the top. Don't stretch it, but neither should you leave it slack or the apples will flatten down as they cook. Press the pastry over to the edges and tuck under slightly, pressing down onto the dish. Pinch the edge to make a crimped pattern. Make a couple of slits in the top for the steam to escape. Brush the top with milk and scatter generously with sugar.

Bake in a hot oven (200°C/400°F) for 5 minutes, then turn down to moderate (180°C/350°F) and cook a further 45 minutes, or until the crust is light brown and the apples tender. If colouring too much, loosely cover the top of the pastry with foil.

Serves 8

Apricot Tart

This style of tart may not be so much in favour these days, with cream and eggs considered undesirable, or downright sinful. But the combination of creamy lightly-set custard over fresh-tasting fruit is exceptionally good. Other fruits can be substituted. Try pears, plums or peaches. The flavour is fresher if you don't poach the fresh fruit first, but you must use ripe fruit or it would remain too hard.

It really doesn't need any accompaniment. A little extra cream could be placed alongside if you feel indulgent.

PASTRY

(Makes enough for a 23cm (9″) pie dish)

1 ¼ cups plain flour

1 tbsp caster sugar

pinch salt

100 g (3 ½ oz) butter

1 egg yolk

a little lemon juice if necessary

The pastry can be made by hand or in the food processor. Mix the flour, sugar and pinch of salt together. Cut the butter into small pieces and mix through until crumbly, bind with egg yolk and, if not moist, add a little lemon juice. Knead for a few seconds until smooth. Wrap in some plastic wrap or waxed paper and leave to rest for 20 minutes.

Roll out and line into a lightly buttered pie plate. Trim the edge level with the dish. If you want a decorative rim push it up slightly and then pinch this to make a neat edge.

Prick the sides and base and bake in a moderate oven (180°C/350°F) for about 25 minutes, or until golden. Don't let it brown, but it should be well-cooked. Leave to cool before placing in the apricots and filling so it will remain crisp.

FILLING

500 g (1 lb) ripe apricots
2 eggs
½ cup (4 fl oz) cream
½ cup sugar
2 tbsp cornflour (cornstarch)
1 tbsp brandy
a little icing sugar to finish the tart

Rinse the apricots and dry them. Cut into halves, remove the stone and then cut into quarters. Arrange these over the base of the tart, skin side down so they are packed fairly firmly. If they are very tiny apricots you could leave them in halves although it makes it harder to cut the finished tart in slices without them pulling away untidily.

Place the eggs, cream, sugar, cornflour and brandy into a bowl and whisk for about 30 seconds, and pour over the top. The filling should come just to the top. If you have difficulty carrying it, half fill on the bench and then top up when the tart is in the oven.

Bake at a moderate temperature (180°C/350°F) for 25–30 minutes until the filling is set. It is fine if it is still a little creamy soft in the centre, as it will be much nicer to eat if not baked too firmly.

Leave to cool for about 10 minutes and sift a little icing sugar over the top before serving. It is nicest served warm. It can be reheated, but if you plan to do this don't sift the top with icing sugar when you first take it from the oven.

Serves 8

Meringue Cases (page 66) filled with cream and a selection of fruit.

Meringue Lemon Cake (page 87).

Rhubarb pie

If rhubarb is coarse and stringy it can be horrible, but it seems to be at its nicest in a pie; the flavour is intense and is enhanced by orange and cinnamon. The filling can be made several days ahead.

Use a spoon when serving this dessert. There will be plenty of delicious juices which you can spoon over each serving so as not to waste a scrap. A jug of running or lightly whipped cream can be placed on the table, for those who like cream with fruit pies.

FILLING

1 orange

½ cup (4 fl oz) orange juice

500 g (1 lb) rhubarb

small piece cinnamon stick

Remove all the rind and pith from the orange.

Cut the flesh into thin slices and then into tiny pieces.

Place into a pan with the remaining ingredients and cook gently, covered for about 10 minutes, or until tender. If there is lots of juice in the pan, turn up the heat and cook until it reduces away. Cool. You can prepare and leave the rhubarb filling for several days.

PASTRY

125 g (4 oz) butter

¼ cup sugar

1 tbsp hot water

1 cup flour

½ cup self-raising flour

pinch salt

Butter a pie dish, 23 cm (9″) in diameter.

Cream the butter with sugar until fluffy and add the hot water.

Sift in the two types of flour and salt and mix well. It should bind together; if not, add a spoonful of milk. Wrap in some plastic wrap or waxed paper and leave to rest in a cool place for about 20 minutes, or place in the refrigerator if the kitchen is warm. Divide the pastry into two: one-third for the top of the pie and the large portion for the base. Roll out the large piece and press into the pie plate.

Fill with the rhubarb, spreading it level. Be sure there is plenty of pastry above the edge of the fruit filling so you can join with the top crust.

Roll out the second portion of pastry and place on top of the rhubarb. Pinch both the edges together and trim away any excess as you go. This is a very easy pastry to handle.

TO FINISH

2 tbsp cream *sugar*

Brush the top with cream; and scatter the sugar over this quite thickly. It will make a lovely crusty, sugary coating.

Bake in a moderate oven (180°C/350°F) until it is golden and the crust quite biscuity to touch. This usually takes about 35 minutes. Don't serve straight from the oven; the rhubarb will be bubbling and too hot. Leave to cool for about 5 minutes before you cut it.

You can reheat but, if the pastry is well-baked, place some foil on top so it won't darken further. Then heat in a moderate oven until warmed through, but not bubbling hot.

Serves 8

PERFUMED FRUIT TART

The most commonly served style of fruit tart has a crisp crust, and a layer of pastry cream topped by glazed fruit. Served cold, it's a rich highly-fattening dessert, frowned on by the cholesterolly-conscious.

The one which I prefer to serve differs in that the fruit is placed directly into the cooked pastry base over a glaze. It is then put into the oven for a very short time, not to cook it but just to warm the fruit. This brings out a wonderful flavour and perfume.

You will need luscious ripe fruits in season. It does need assembling close to serving time, but I can promise you it is worth that last-minute loving attention.

The pastry in this recipe is light and crisp, and one of the nicest of all for any fruit tart, mince pie, cheesecake — or whatever you may wish to fill it with.

PASTRY

[Makes enough for a base 23 cm (9″), either round or oblong]

1½ cups plain flour
pinch salt
2 tbsp caster sugar
125 g (4 oz) unsalted butter
1 egg yolk
a few drops of either almond or vanilla essence
1 tbsp water

You can make this pastry by hand or in a food processor. Either way it is very successful.

Mix the flour, salt and sugar together. Cut the butter into small pieces and either work it into the flour mixture with your hands or process until it is in crumb-sized bits.

Add the egg yolk, almond or vanilla essence and water, and work the flour and butter until it holds together when you press a little piece together in your fingers. If dry, add another teaspoon or two of water. Gather it up into a ball and wrap in some plastic wrap. Leave to rest for about 30 minutes (or you can freeze it for up to 4 weeks).

Roll out the pastry. I like to do this between waxed greaseproof paper or plastic wrap so no additional flour needs to be used on the bench. (This can alter the proportions of the mixture.)

Press the pastry over the base and sides of a flan tin and cut level with the top edge. Be sure the edges are even and, for a fruit tart, not too wafer-thin. You can patch if necessary. If at all sticky, chill in the dish until firm.

Lightly brush the shiny side of some foil with butter and press over the base and up the sides. Bake in a moderate oven (180°C/350°F) until the base has set. This usually takes about 20 minutes. Carefully remove the foil and return to the oven until the pastry is a light golden brown, and crisp.

Remove and cool in the tin. It is best left like this until you are ready to add the fruit. When you put the fruit in, place the pastry onto a flat baking tray.

FILLING

¾ cup red currant jelly
1 tbsp kirsch
2 punnets (500 g/1 lb) small strawberries
1 punnet (250 g/8 oz) raspberries
½ cup blueberries, blackberries or other dark, ripe berry

Heat the jelly and kirsch together until bubbling. Brush a layer over the pre-baked pastry shell. Let it set. You can do this hours before filling with the fruit.

Hull the strawberries. Check the raspberries, putting them onto a flat bench so you can discard any bruised or mouldy ones that sometimes sneak into a punnet. Arrange the strawberries, beginning from the outside of the tart, resting each one against its neighbour.

When you have about 2–3 layers, arrange the raspberries, and finally the dark blueberries or other berries in the centre. Once this is done it can be left a couple of hours unless the berries are too soft. Any longer and the juices may begin to leak into the base and soften it.

Just before serving, put the tart into a moderate oven (180°C/350°F) for about 8 minutes. It will warm the fruit slightly and make it perfumed. Warm the rest of the red currant jelly. If it has become too sticky, add a spoonful of water or kirsch. Dab just a little over the top of the berries quickly before taking it to the table.

Serves 8

VARIATION: PEACH OR NECTARINE TART

¾ cup apricot jam | *6 peaches or nectarines*

Substitute apricot jam for the red currant jelly and 6 peaches or nectarines (depending of course on their size) for the berries. They should be ripe but not mushy. Leave the skin on the nectarines. You can peel the peaches if you wish.

Brush the tart base with the jam and cut the fruit into slices down towards the stone, removing this. Arrange them in the tart base, slightly overlapping. This tart needs to be heated and served once made or the fruit will discolour. If you scatter with a little lemon juice it will help prevent this happening but not too much or you will make the base too wet. Put into the oven for 8 minutes to warm slightly. Have the apricot jam warming and brush just a little here and there on top of the fruit to give it a shine.

PECAN PIE

President Lincoln was not particularly interested in food according to his biographer William Harden, who commented, 'Abe Lincoln can sit and think longer without food than any man I know'. He did, however, have a weakness for desserts and when he moved to Washington a city baker, who specialised in pecan pies, declared Lincoln was one of his most regular customers.

Pecan pie is sweet and rich so don't serve too large a portion. Usually pecans are left whole — it looks more attractive — but makes the pie more difficult to cut neatly. So always be sure to use a very sharp knife.

PASTRY

185 g (6 oz) flour
125 g (4 oz) butter
2 tbsp caster sugar
1 small egg

This can be made by hand or in a food processor. Place the flour into a bowl. Chop the butter into pieces and add, and process or crumble with your fingertips. Add the sugar and egg, and mix or process to a paste. If you use a food processor it is usually softer than mixing by hand. If you *are* mixing by hand, knead for a few seconds. Wrap the pastry and chill several hours. Roll out and press into a flan tin or pie tin, 23 cm (9″) in diameter.

Lightly butter a piece of foil and press, buttered side down, into the case. Bake in a moderate oven (180°C/350°F) for 15 minutes, or until set. Remove the foil and cook a further 4–5 minutes until dry. Don't let the pastry colour at this stage.

FILLING

3 eggs
1 cup (8 fl oz) dark corn syrup
⅓ cup sugar
30 g (1 oz) butter, melted
1 tsp vanilla
1½ cups pecan nuts
1 tbsp cocoa

Beat the eggs with the corn syrup, sugar, butter and vanilla. Stir through the nuts. Sift the cocoa over the top and mix.

Pour into the pastry shell. The mixture should come to the top. If the nuts are not even move them around until you have a good layer.

Place into a moderate oven (180°C/350°F) and bake for 45 minutes, or until set. If you like a sticky pie leave the centre on the soft side. It will firm more as it cools but will remain very moist.

Serves 8–10

ORANGE DREAM TART

Golden pieces of candied orange have a great deal of character in their flavour and texture: tender, yet at the same time, firm; sweet but sharp. This lovely creamy tart combines the nicest of all tastes: tart orange with sweetness; rich cream and butter; and the texture of crisp light base and a soft filling.

A good cognac (instead of Grand Marnier) is also marvellous with the orange for the filling. This dessert is best eaten on the day it is made. I like it garnished with a few perfectly trimmed orange segments on the side.

PASTRY

[Makes enough for a tart base 23 cm (9") in diameter]

1 cup plain flour
pinch salt
90 g (3 oz) unsalted butter
1 or 2 tbsp dry white wine, lemon juice or water

Sift the flour and salt into a bowl (you could use a food processor). Chop the butter into tiny pieces and add. Either crumble the mixture with your fingers until in tiny pieces throughout, or else process until crumbly. If making by hand it is much easier if you use butter which is not refrigerator-cold. Add the dry white wine, one tablespoon should be enough in a food processor. You might need a little more if mixing by hand. Process until it forms a ball, or if by hand, tip out onto your bench and, using the heel of the hand, smear the pastry away from you across the bench and it will blend together. Gather up again, form into a round, flat shape and wrap in plastic wrap. Leave to rest for 20 minutes. Refrigerate only if the kitchen is very hot.

Roll out between some waxed paper or on a very lightly-floured board. Now put into the flan tin, pressing on the base and up the edges. Trim any excess away. Prick the base with a fork and chill for about 30 minutes.

Brush some foil with a little melted butter on one side. Press, buttered side down, onto the base and up the sides.

Put into a moderately hot oven (200°C/400°F) for 5 minutes, then reduce the oven to moderate (180°C/350°F) and cook for a further 12–15 minutes, or until the base is set. Carefully peel away the foil and continue baking until it has become dry and crisp, usually another 7–10 minutes.

FILLING

1 medium-sized orange	*2 eggs*
½ cup sugar	*1 tbs sugar*
¼ cup (2 fl oz) Grand Marnier	*⅓ cup cream*
1 cup sultanas	

Don't peel the orange but cut it (skin and all) into thin horizontal slices, discarding any pips. Now dice these slices, including skin and pith, and place in a saucepan. Cover generously with cold water and bring to the boil and cook for about 5 minutes. Drain and discard this water which will be quite bitter.

Cover generously with fresh water and cook gently until the orange rind is tender. Turn up the heat and boil until there are just a few spoonfuls of liquid in the base of the pan. Add the sugar and cook until syrupy. But watch closely; it can burn easily if left.

Put into a basin, add the Grand Marnier and sultanas, and stir. Cover and leave to marinate for 24 hours. All the liquid should be absorbed.

Beat the eggs with the additional tablespoon of sugar and add the cream. Mix into the orange and sultanas.

Pour the orange filling into the baked, hot crust and return to the oven. Cook until the edges are firm, they will be golden brown and beginning to puff slightly. The centre shouldn't be runny, but can still be slightly on the creamy side. It will firm more as the tart cools a little. It usually takes about 30 minutes, but rely on the look and touch rather than timing.

Even if you intend to serve this hot, leave to sit for 10 minutes before cutting. It can be eaten cold or warm, but don't refrigerate. It is best served at room temperature. If you want to reheat the tart, put into a moderate oven for about 8 minutes to warm just a little.

Serves 8

RED CURRANT TART

The thickened buttery egg and fruit mixture which is the filling for this tart dates back to the 17th century. Country housewives cooked fresh fruits for the stillroom in summer, so they could enjoy fruity fillings in their tarts during winter months. Lemons, oranges, passionfruit and even apricots can be used.

Intensely flavoured fruits are the most successful. This is why red currant is so good. It makes a bright pink curd.

The pastry is sweet and 'shortbread'. To retain the crunchy texture fill only an hour before eating. Keep any garnishing simple: just cream and a couple of red currants, or perhaps a tiny scrap of angelica.

TART BASES

1 cup flour
90 g (3 oz) butter
pinch salt
3 tbsp icing sugar (confectioner's sugar)
1 egg yolk
few drops vanilla essence

Put the flour onto a clean bench-top, make a well in the centre and into this put the butter, chopped into small pieces, salt, icing sugar and egg yolks. Flavour with vanilla. It is easiest to mix if the butter is not too hard. Using your fingers mix up the centre ingredients. This may be a bit messy but it's the best way to get a lovely texture in the biscuit pastry. Work in the flour from the edges and mix to a paste, kneading lightly until smooth. Wrap in some plastic wrap, leave to rest in a cool part of the kitchen or refrigerator for about 20 minutes. Roll out and cut circles from the pastry, about 7 cm (3″) in size. Place onto a buttered flat baking try. Prick the centre in several places. Bake in a moderate oven (180°C/350°F) until golden. Remove to a rack to cool. Store them in an airtight tin. They keep well about 4 days.

RED CURRANT CURD

250 g (8 oz) red currants
¼ cup (2 fl oz) water
½ cup sugar
45 g (1½ oz) butter
2 egg yolks

Pull the red currants away from the stems and rinse them. Place into a saucepan with the water. Cover the pan and cook very gently until soft. Push through a sieve, pressing down to get as much juice as possible. Measure. You should have about ½ cup (4 fl oz). If you have much more than this, reduce again over the heat, or the curd will not be thick enough. Mix the sugar into the red currants and place in a small saucepan. Warm for a few minutes to dissolve the sugar. Chop the butter into pieces, add and stir. Whisk the yolks, add a little of the hot liquid to them, return to the heat and stir until lightly thickened. Don't let it boil. It will thicken more as it cools. Stir occasionally while cooling and refrigerate.

Try to make this 12 hours before you use the curd so it will thicken nicely. Refrigerated, it can be kept for about 2 weeks.

TO ASSEMBLE

1 cup cream

a few sprigs of fresh red currants for each tart

Whip the cream until it holds firm peaks. Don't sweeten as the curd provides sufficient sweetness. Pipe a circle of cream around the edge of each tart. Fill with the red currant curd and arrange a few red currants on the side. If you find the curd very firm, you may find it easier to spread it on the tart base first, then pipe around the edge.

Once assembled, eat within about 4 hours or the tarts begin to soften. If you have the cream whipped ready and red currants sorted out on a plate for decorations, the tarts take only a couple of minutes to assemble.

This tart can also be made with lemon butter or lemon curd, and makes a lovely 'shortbread' base for fresh berries.

Makes 12 tarts 7 cm (3″) in size

APPLE AND BLUEBERRY UPSIDE DOWN TART

When this tart is served it is a surprise to find the soft apple stained a purple colour from juices of the blueberries. Bound in a creamy ground almond custard on the base, the thin, light buttery crust on top completely conceals them.

Its preparation is really no different from that of a conventional tart, but it is an interesting variation. I've found it much easier to turn out a glass or china pie dish than a metal one because sometimes the juicy filling bubbles on the edges and caramelises. This sticks to metal and can only be removed with difficulty.

You can make it purely with apples when blueberries are not in season although frozen blueberries are quite successful, but they leave more juices. Serve with thick cream, either running or lightly whipped.

PASTRY

1 cup flour
pinch salt
90 g (3 oz) butter
2 egg yolks
1 tbsp lemon juice

Lightly butter a pie dish, 20 cm (8″), but not too shallow. It should be about 10 cm (2″) high.

You can either make the pastry in a food processor or by hand. Sift the flour and salt together. Chop the butter into a few pieces and add. Process or crumble quickly with your fingers until it is mixed through. Mix to a dough with egg yolks and lemon juice, kneading for a minute. Wrap in a piece of waxed paper or plastic wrap and leave to rest at room temperature for 20 minutes, or in the refrigerator if the kitchen is warm. It can be stored chilled for several days.

Roll out between sheets of waxed paper and put into the lightly buttered pie dish. Don't fold the pastry over the edge as you will want to turn the dish out once cooked.

FILLING

500 g (1 lb) cooking apples, peeled, cored and sliced thinly
60 g (2 oz) butter
3 tbsp sugar
250 g (8 oz) blueberries

Put the apples into a saucepan with the butter and sugar. Cook very gently, stirring every so often until they are soft and slightly glazed, with gold tinges on the edges. Once they begin to caramelise, watch them carefully. They can catch at this stage if you don't stir or turn them. Remove from the heat and mix in the blueberries. Stir gently. Let the fruit cool and put into the pastry case.

Place into a moderate oven (180°C/350°F) and let it cook until the pastry is golden. This usually takes about 25–30 minutes.

TOPPING

1 egg
60 g (2 oz) ground almonds
1 tsp vanilla essence
3 tbsp icing sugar (confectioner's sugar)
½ cup (4 fl oz) cream

Beat all the topping ingredients together for 30 seconds. When the tart base is nicely coloured, pour the topping over the fruit and bake for a further 15 minutes, or until it has barely set in the centre. Don't let it cook until it puffs up and becomes firm. Remove from the oven and leave to cool for about 5–10 minutes. Invert onto a plate (unless the syrup from the apples has boiled over the edge and made it sticky the pastry will slide out easily), so the filling is on the plate and the pale brown biscuit casing on top.

Sift a little icing sugar over the tart and serve cut into wedges while still warm.

If you make it during the day it can be warmed again but try and invert it onto an ovenproof plate as it is impossible to move. About 15 minutes in a moderate oven should be enough time. Leave the dusting of icing sugar over the top until it has heated up.

Serves 8

CHERRY CREAM CHEESE TART

An especially nice cheese tart with a crunchy coconut and nut base under a thin cheese topping, coloured a little with cherry juices. Don't use a sour cherry, a sweet eating cherry is best. When cherries are not in season this tart can be made using canned cherries. Be sure to pip them and don't cook, as in this recipe. Add to the cream cheese with a little brandy and, as they will be juicier than fresh cooked ones, don't use any of the syrup or it will be too wet.

BASE

¼ cup desiccated coconut
½ cup ground walnuts
¼ cup caster sugar
½ cup ground almonds
45 g (1½ oz) butter

Mix all the ingredients except the butter. Now melt the butter and add the dry ingredients to the saucepan. It is easiest to mix thoroughly this way. Stir well and press onto the base (but not up the sides) of a lightly buttered flan tin, 23 cm (9″) in size. Bake in a moderate oven (180°C/350°F) for about 10–12 minutes. Leave to cool.

FILLING

45 g (1½ oz) butter
¼ cup sugar
250 g (8 oz) stoned fresh cherries
1 tbsp brandy
250 g (8 oz) cream cheese
2 egg yolks
grated rind 1 lemon
2 egg whites

Melt the butter with sugar in a frying pan. Add the cherries and cook over fairly high heat, stirring until a syrup has formed around them. They should be tender but not too soft. If they are caramelising too much and no liquid is forming, place a lid on the pan for a few minutes. Add the brandy. Pour through a sieve to drain, but keep the syrup. Measure it. If more than a third of a cup remains, reduce in the pan. But see that it doesn't burn as it will be quite thick.

Cream or process the cream cheese until smooth, mix with yolks, lemon rind and juice from the cherries.

Beat the whites until stiff and fold through the mixture, about a third at a time. Place the mixture in the flan tin and spread out over the base. Put the cherries on top. The best way is simply to drop them evenly onto the cheese. They will sink through, although a few little bits of pink may show here and there.

Bake in a moderate oven until the top is set, it will firm more as it cools but usually takes about 40 minutes.

Leave to cool and then store refrigerated if not eating the day you make it. Remove about an hour before eating or it is too firm and hard.

Serves 8

Almond Caramel Tarts in Coconut Pastry

The base of these tarts is light and buttery with a slight crunchiness from the coconut. The filling is a sticky golden caramel which could include almonds, macadamia or pecan nuts.

COCONUT PASTRY

1 cup flour
2 tbsp icing sugar
90 g (3 oz) butter
2 tbsp desiccated coconut
1 small egg

You can make this either by hand or in a food processor. Mix the flour and icing sugar together. Chop the butter into a few pieces and either crumble with your fingers until in small pieces, or process. Add the coconut and stir through. Then mix to a paste with the egg. If mixed in a food processor, it will be quite moist. Wrap and chill for several hours. It is not quite so moist if made by hand, but if it's difficult to roll, chilling helps.

Roll out between some waxed paper and cut into rounds, slightly larger than the tart cases. Press firmly into each case and onto the sides. Prick the base in several places. Place the cases on a flat baking sheet and cook in a moderate oven (180°C/350°F) until they are lightly coloured. Rely on the look of the pastry rather than timing, but it takes about 20 minutes.

Remove and cool in the container in which they were baked. It is best to fill them in these, and then remove later. They will come out easily.

ALMOND CARAMEL FILLING

250 g (8 oz) almond slivers or roughly chopped blanched almonds
¾ cup sugar
⅓ cup (3 fl oz) water
¾ cup (6 fl oz) cream

Toast the almonds on a tray in the oven until lightly coloured. Be careful as they can burn easily. They usually take about 5 minutes, and will smell nutty when they are ready.

Heat the sugar and water gently until the sugar has dissolved, turn up the heat and cook until a golden caramel has formed. Add the cream immediately, before the mixture becomes dark, and cook until the toffee has dissolved to form a caramel sauce. Add the almonds and stir. Don't let it cool. You need to fill the cases while the caramel is warm or it will set too firmly.

Leave to set in a cool place, not the refrigerator. They can be served plain or decorated with chocolate.

TO DECORATE

100 g (3½ oz) dark sweet chocolate (optional)

Break the chocolate into pieces and place either into a double boiler or a basin over hot water. Warm until melted and stir. Fill into a piping bag with a plain writing tube and pipe a lattice or decorate with random strips on top of each tart. Let set. These are nicest eaten within 24 hours of making.

Makes 8 tarts, 7.5 cm (3") in diameter

MERINGUE CASES

There are numerous ways you can use meringue cases: fill with any fruits in season, with curds such as lemon, orange or the red currant one in this book, mounded with flavoured ice-creams, or even simply with a heap of snowy cream rising from the centre. They keep for several weeks in an airtight tin, so are a good dessert to keep on hand.

2 egg whites
pinch salt
¼ tsp cream of tartar
⅓ cup caster sugar
½ tsp vanilla essence

Line a baking sheet with non-stick baking paper. Beat the egg whites with salt and cream of tartar until stiff. Gradually add the sugar, beating until very stiff. Flavour with vanilla.

Use half the mixture to make 8 circles, a spoon will flatten these out evenly. Put the remaining meringue into a pastry bag fitted with a star tube and pipe around the edge of each circle, keeping it well inside so you have a casing.

Bake the meringue cases in a slow oven (120°C/250°F) until they are crisp to touch and creamy in colour. If they are beginning to colour too much turn off the oven and let them stand with the door closed to crisp up.

Cool on a baking sheet on a wire rack and, as soon as they are cool, carefully remove them from the paper and store in an airtight tin.

Makes 8 cases

LEMON TART

Always among the most popular flavourings for a tart, an ideal lemon filling should be velvety and creamy, yet should leave a sharp, fresh taste. Lemons vary in acid considerably. Eurekas or Lisbons are suitable, but Meyer lemons are not as tart and sharp. Be careful not to grate any of the white pith when preparing the rind; it will make the filling taste bitter.

A slice can be accompanied by a small mound of berries alongside, or served quite plain.

PASTRY

[Makes enough for a 20 cm (8") tart base]

1 cup flour
2 tbsp caster sugar
90 g (3 oz) butter
1 egg yolk
2 tsp lemon juice

This pastry can be made either in a food processor or by hand. Place the flour and sugar in a bowl or processor. Add the butter cut into a few pieces and either crumble by hand, or process, until crumbly. Add the egg yolk and lemon juice and mix to a dough. If too dry, add a little more lemon juice. If making by hand, knead for a moment.

Wrap in some waxed paper or plastic wrap and leave to rest in a cool place for about 20 minutes. Roll out and place into a lightly buttered flan tin with a removable base, pressing firmly on the edges.

To make a small edge, trim the dough where it comes to the top of the rim of the flan tin and then press the sides up just a tiny bit more, using two fingers. Pinch between thumb and index finger all the way round. Prick the base. Press a piece of foil, with the inside lightly buttered, over the pastry and cook in a moderate oven (180°C/350°F) for about 20–25 minutes or until golden, without browning. Remove the foil and let the shell cool completely. If you add the lemon filling while it is warm it becomes soft.

FILLING

3 eggs
¾ cup caster sugar
grated rind 2 large lemons
⅓ cup lemon juice
½ cup (4 fl oz) cream

Whisk together the eggs, sugar, lemon rind and juice until the mixture is frothy. Add cream to the lemon and whisk again.

Place the baked pastry case onto a flat oven tray and half-fill with the lemon. Put this into a moderate oven (180°C/350°F) and fill with the remaining mixture. It may be easier if you transfer it to a jug to do this. (It is very difficult to move the tart without spilling the filling if you pour it all in before placing the tart in the oven. If this happens it will then stick to the edges of the case and caramelise.)

Cook for 30 minutes or until firm on the edges but still a little wobbly in the centre. Check by lightly shaking the tart shell. As it cools it will firm more. It will be creamy in colour.

While tepid remove from the flan tin or it can stick, and leave to cool completely.

Serves 8

Cheese Cake

There seem to be a million recipes for cheese cakes. Mostly they fall into two categories: a baked Continental style, or one made by creaming the cheese and mixing it with gelatine so it will set. I tried this latter version with some misgivings some years ago. It is made with eggs which are whipped until frothy and folded through the cheese.

Despite not being cooked, it tastes like a baked cake, but lighter.

Cheese cake is usually a little cloying because of the soft, full fat cheese. The lemon helps cut through this. It is still a little too rich for my taste, so serve some fruit alongside, and cut it in smallish portions.

CRUST

60 g (2 oz) butter
1 tsp ground cinnamon
250 g (8 oz) plain sweet biscuits

Apple and Blueberry Upside Down Tart (page 61)
and Almond Caramel Tarts in Coconut Pastry (page 65).

Christmas Fluff (page 83)
and Almond Wafers (page 129).

Lightly butter a spring form tin, 30 cm (12″) in size.

Crush the butter into a few pieces and leave to melt. Crush the biscuits, add cinnamon and mix with the butter. Tip into the tin and press out to make a casing. It should stick together although it won't be very moist. You will find it easier if you press this onto the sides first, and then thin the crumbs by brushing some away. Be sure not to have it too thick. Thin down the crumbs where the base meets the sides.

Bake in a moderate oven (180°C/350°F) for 10–15 minutes, or until a toasted, pale brown. Cool.

FILLING

1 tbsp gelatine
¼ cup (2 fl oz) water
500 g (1 lb) cream cheese
60 g (2 oz) unsalted butter
grated rind 1 large lemon
¼ cup (2 fl oz) lemon juice
½ tsp nutmeg
3 eggs
¾ cup caster sugar
¾ cup (6 fl oz) cream

Mix the gelatine and water and dissolve.

Cream the cream cheese and the unsalted butter until fluffy. Add the lemon rind and juice, and the nutmeg and mix through. Separate the eggs.

Beat the yolks with sugar until fluffy. Add the gelatine. Mix in the cream cheese.

Whip the whites and, when stiff, beat the cream until it holds soft peaks. Mix them both together and fold into the cream cheese. Place into the case, smoothing out until level. If you have taken the crumbs too high, brush these onto the edges.

Leave to set in the refrigerator for about 8 hours or until firm. You can serve plain or decorate around the edges with whole strawberries or other berry fruits.

Serves 10–12

COLD PUDDINGS

Flummeries, bavarois, fruit fools, syllabub, creams — these are just some of the wonderful cold puddings which became famous in Tudor times, elaborately decorated and served with great style. The modern versions of these cold sweets are simpler, with a little less cream and fewer eggs, and the decorations are kept minimal, so the effect is pretty and fresh.

In those recipes that have gelatine, I have kept it to a minimum, wherever possible. By using only enough gelatine to set lightly means the dessert can be kept covered and refrigerated for a couple of days, without becoming leathery.

Gelatine, which is in a number of these desserts, must be measured very accurately. Use either a metric or imperial spoon, according to which measure you are using, but never a kitchen one, and be sure the measurements are all level. In most recipes I think it is best always to mix the dry gelatine granules with liquid in a cup. Stir to mix all the dry pieces and dissolve by standing the cup in a pan of simmering water.

There are so many delicious cold desserts you can make that it was difficult to decide which ones to include, but this selection covers a range of flavourings and styles. See also Old-fashioned Puddings on page 100.

SPICY MOUSSE

A great party dish because you can whip it together with speed — no cooking is required — and it keeps for several days. If you want to serve some fruit with the mousse, poached apples or pears are best, or those fruits which have an affinity with the sort of spices flavouring the mousse. If you are having only a few people for dinner, you can halve the recipe successfully.

1 tbsp gelatine

⅓ cup (2½ fl oz) water

¼ cup (2 fl oz) lemon juice

6 eggs

1 cup caster sugar

2 tbsp brandy

½ tsp ground ginger

1 tsp ground cinnamon

1 tsp ground nutmeg

1 tsp vanilla essence

1½ cups (12 fl oz) cream

Put the gelatine into a cup, add water and stir. Stand in a saucepan with hot water and heat until the gelatine has dissolved. Meanwhile, beat the eggs in a large bowl with the sugar until they are very thick, fluffy and pale. You really need an electric beater; it is very tedious if you have to do this by hand.

Add the lemon juice and brandy to the gelatine. Stir in the spices and vanilla; they should fit into the cup. Mix this into the eggs.

Whip the cream until it holds soft peaks and fold through. Pour into a large bowl with a capacity of 12 cups and chill until set. It firms quite quickly and can be served in a couple of hours.

You can keep it refrigerated for up to 48 hours, covered over with plastic wrap.

Serves 12 generously

Norwegian Pudding

Despite its name, this pudding has no links with Norway. A recipe which originally came from the Cordon Bleu cooking school in London, I've made it for years with great success, but without knowing why it was so named. A nicer pudding than it may sound, the combination of apricot, very light custard, chocolate and cream is not as rich as it would appear. It is best served very cold.

½ cup (4 fl oz) apricot jam
2 cups (16 fl oz) milk
1 egg
3 egg yolks
3 tbsp sugar
½ tsp vanilla essence
90 g (3 oz) dark sweetened chocolate, grated
½ cup (4 fl oz) cream
1 egg white

If the jam is lumpy, push through a sieve. You will find it even easier if you warm it slightly first. Spread out evenly so it covers the base. The dish should hold 4–5 cups, and if you use one which is shallow rather than deep it is nicer, both to serve and eat — with a light scattering of chocolate and cream over each portion.

Heat the milk and, while it is warming, beat the egg and yolks with sugar and vanilla. Pour over the hot milk, stirring as you do so, and then pour over the apricot jam in the dish. Place the dish in a pan which has sufficient hot water to come about halfway up the sides. If you can't move the dish easily, put it in the oven, and then fill with a jug. Bake until lightly set and leave to cool.

Scatter the grated chocolate evenly over the top.

Whip the cream until it holds soft peaks, and whip the egg white until stiff. Fold them both together. Place into spoonfuls all over the top of the dessert, and spread out with a knife. You won't disturb the chocolate coating as much this way.

Chill again. It's best left about 4 hours, but it keeps well for 24.

Serves 6

MARBLED SOUFFLE

This is a pretty dish, not too rich or heavy. The plain bavarois mixture provides a foil for the richer chocolate portions.

1 tbsp and 2 tsp gelatine
1/3 cup water
1 1/2 cups (12 fl oz) milk
7 egg yolks
1 cup caster sugar
1 tsp vanilla essence
5 egg whites
1/2 cup (4 fl oz) cream
60 g (2 oz) dark sweetened chocolate
1/4 cup (2 fl oz) milk
2 tsp instant coffee
2 tbsp dark rum

If you want this to look like a soufflé, choose a dish which holds 4 cups so the mixture will rise well above the edge.

Lightly oil a strip of foil which will fit around the dish, and tie firmly near the top, so the foil extends above. If the foil is not a heavy variety, you will need to use a double thickness.

Mix the gelatine with water, then warm in a cup standing in hot water until dissolved.

Warm the milk in a saucepan. While it is heating beat the yolks with sugar until thick and fluffy. Gradually add the milk and return to the heat. Stir with a whisk until the custard is lightly thickened. Don't let it boil.

Add the gelatine and vanilla and leave to cool, giving it an occasional stir.

When cold, beat the whites until stiff and fold through the custard, about a third at a time.

Whip the cream until it holds very soft peaks, and fold in. Now pour the mixture into two bowls, halving as evenly as possible.

Place the chocolate with milk and instant coffee into a small saucepan. Warm, with a lid on the pan, over the very lowest heat until the chocolate is melted. If you can't keep the flame low, heat in a basin standing over a pan of simmering water. Add to one of the bowls of custard.

Chill until the mixture becomes slightly jellied. Don't let it set too much or, when you place into the soufflé dish to marble, it will form little mounds which give it an uneven top.

Place a spoonful of each mixture into the soufflé dish, at random. It doesn't matter if some spoonfuls are more generous than others; it adds to the effect if it doesn't look too 'perfect'. Refrigerate until set.

Remove the foil collar carefully before serving. You can decorate the top with a few rosettes of whipped cream around the edge and a little grated chocolate scattered over this, if you wish.

Serves 8

PINK JELLY MOULDS

Under a children's birthday-party menu in the *Harrods Book of Entertaining* is a recipe for Jelly Mountains: strawberry jelly with fresh puréed strawberries. It is surprisingly good. Even better, I find, if a sharper jelly such as raspberry is used and if much less sugar is added. It is suggested in the recipe that you could sieve the berry pulp. I don't do that because I like the more textured taste of the strawberries with a few bits of purée and pips. But, of course, you can please yourself.

A deceptive dish, it tastes more complex than it is to make. It's good for occasions when time is extra precious. I think it needs cream, but I always like jelly and cream together.

250 g (8 oz) strawberries
1 tbsp sugar
1 raspberry jelly
half the quantity of water recommended on the jelly instructions
1 tbsp lemon juice

Hull the berries, and cut them into halves if large. Add the sugar and stir. Leave to marinate for about 1 hour or until juices have formed around them.

Purée the berries in a food processor or blender.

Make up the jelly with just half the quantity of liquid and add lemon juice.

Measure the berries, mix into the jelly and stir well. If this mixture does not equal the quantity of liquid recommended on the jelly packet, add water.

Pour into a mould, or into 4 individual dishes or wine glasses and chill until set.

You can serve them with a rosette of cream on top so they look like a party sweet, or with a little running cream trickled over the top.

Serves 4

TWO-TONED CHOCOLATE ORANGE FANTASY

A very good party sweet, you can easily double the quantity. It can be prepared several days beforehand and is easy to make — despite its appearance. The orange lightens the richness of the chocolate, and you can serve some fresh orange segments alongside.

90 g (3 oz) dark sweet eating chocolate
3 eggs, separated
6 tbsp icing sugar (confectioner's sugar)
grated rind 1 large, or 2 small oranges
few drops orange flower water
3 tsp gelatine
¼ cup (2 fl oz) orange juice
2 tbsp Grand Marnier
1 tbsp brandy
1½ cups (12 fl oz) cream

Break the chocolate into pieces and put into a basin. Stand over or in a pan of warm water and leave over a gentle heat to melt while you are preparing the dessert.

Beat the egg yolks with sugar and orange rind, mix in orange flower water.

Mix the gelatine with orange juice and dissolve. The best way is to place in a cup and stand this in simmering water. Meanwhile, whip the cream until it holds soft peaks, and beat the egg whites until stiff. Add the gelatine to the yolks. Stir to mix thoroughly.

Mix the cream with the egg yolks and, lastly, fold in the whites, a third at a time. Take out 1 cup of the mixture and place into a separate bowl. Mix the melted chocolate into this. If it becomes streaky and uneven you can place it back into the warmed bowl the chocolate was originally melted in, and it should become smooth.

TO ASSEMBLE

Place ½ cup of orange mixture into a crystal or glass dish, then ¼ cup of chocolate in the centre of this. It will just naturally spread out and form layers. Continue, making about 3 layers, until you have used up both the orange and chocolate.

Cover with some plastic wrap and refrigerate until set. It will take only a couple of hours.

Although it keeps for about 3 days, it is nicest eaten within 48 hours. Decorate with some thin slices of peeled orange or orange segments if you wish, but don't add any more cream as decoration. It is quite creamy enough.

Serves 6–8

YOGHURT WITH DRIED FRUITS AND NUTS

Not at all complicated to make, this dessert has a slightly tart flavour which is counteracted by pieces of sweet dried fruits and the crunchiness of toasted nuts.

¼ cup sultanas (golden raisins) cut into halves
1 tbsp glacé cherries, finely chopped
2 tbsp dates, stones removed and fruit finely chopped
2 tsp gelatine
½ cup (4 fl oz) orange juice
1 tbsp lemon juice
⅓ cup brown sugar
2 cups (16 fl oz) unsweetened yoghurt
2 tbsp chopped blanched almonds

Place the fruits into a bowl and cover with boiling water. While making up the dessert, leave them to stand so they will soften.

Mix the gelatine with orange juice and lemon juice and heat in a cup standing in boiling water until dissolved. Stir in brown sugar and yoghurt together. When the gelatine has dissolved add to it a few spoonfuls of the yoghurt mixture, or the gelatine will set too quickly. Then mix in all the yoghurt. Drain the fruits and mix through.

Brown the almonds in a dry frying pan or in the oven, turning them over so they toast evenly. Cool. Mix into the yoghurt and pour the mixture into individual dessert dishes or wine glasses. Stir the fruit through and even it out with a spoon as it tends to sink to the base of the mixing bowl. These set quickly, usually within a couple of hours.

They keep well for 36 hours if stored covered with some plastic wrap.

Serves 4

Two-toned wine jelly

Two-toned, with the burgundy colour of red wine set over a golden white wine jelly, this is an adult dessert. It can be served on its own, with some berries alongside, or with cream, for those who love jelly and cream.

RED WINE JELLY

1 tbsp gelatine
2 cups (16 fl oz) light red wine
4 tbsp lemon juice
2/3 cup sugar
1 tbsp brandy
1 tbsp red currant jelly

Mix the gelatine with 1/2 cup of the red wine and stir. Heat the remainder of the wine with lemon juice and sugar. When the sugar has dissolved, add the gelatine, brandy and red currant jelly and leave until both gelatine and red currant jelly have dissolved. Remove and let cool.

WHITE WINE JELLY

1 tbsp gelatine
2 cups (16 fl oz) sweet white wine
2/3 cup sugar
1 tbsp lemon juice

Mix the gelatine with 1/2 cup of the white wine and stir. Heat the remainder of the wine with sugar and lemon juice and, when the sugar has dissolved, add the gelatine and leave this to dissolve. Remove and let cool.

TO ASSEMBLE

Pour one of the jellies into the dessert dish. It doesn't matter which one is first; I prefer the white jelly on the top and the darker one on the base. Refrigerate the bowl. Keep the other jelly out at room temperature so it won't begin to set.

As soon as the first jelly has become firm, pour the second wine jelly on top. If it has begun to set, you can warm it gently until tepid, but don't pour over the set jelly unless it is cold or it will begin to melt the latter. Chill them both and leave for 12 hours before serving, so the flavours mature.

Cover the bowl while storing. It keeps very well for 48 hours.

Serves 8–10

LIME MOULDS

The variety usually found in shops is a Tahitian lime, small and a bright green colour, with paler green and yellow graduations on the skin. The taste is sharper and more intense than lemon. The colour of lime is part of its charm. If you can't buy limes, lemons could be used.

2 eggs
¾ cup caster sugar
grated rind 1 lime
1 tbsp gelatine
⅓ cup (2½ oz) lime juice
½ cup (4 fl oz) orange juice
1 cup (8 fl oz) cream

Separate the eggs and beat the yolks with sugar and rind of the lime until the eggs are fluffy. Mix the gelatine with lime juice and place cup into a pot with hot water, and leave to dissolve.

Add the orange juice to the gelatine and mix into the egg yolk. Beat the cream until it forms soft peaks and beat the egg whites until they are quite stiff. Fold through the cream and, lastly, the whites, a little at a time.

Pour into a container — use one which holds about 4 cups (36 fl oz) — and leave to set in the refrigerator. Cover if keeping for more than a few hours, it firms up quite quickly and could be served a couple of hours after making it.

I think the flavours improve if it stands for 24 hours. This is a dessert which keeps particularly well, still tasting very fresh 2–3 days later.

It can be decorated with a few slices of strawberry, a little cream and some blanched shreds of lime peel. It is also good accompanied by a berry sauce, although this needs to be a sweetened one as the lime dish is quite tart.

Serves 6 generously

PARIS BREST

A famous classic dessert which has a crisp choux pastry usually filled with a vanilla or chocolate pastry cream. This variation is an easier dish and a lighter dessert, with orange-flavoured whipped cream and fresh strawberries. The circle of choux can be baked several days beforehand and stored in a tin. It should stay crisp, but if it softens at all, five minutes in a moderate oven (180°C/350°F) will crisp it again.

CHOUX PASTRY

60 g (2 oz) butter	*½ cup flour*
½ cup (4 fl oz) water	*2 large eggs*
pinch salt	*1 tbsp flaked almonds*

Butter a flat baking tray. Chop the butter into small pieces and put into a saucepan with the water and salt. Bring slowly to the boil. The idea is to let the butter melt by the time the water has boiled so you won't lose any liquid. While it is heating, sift the flour onto a piece of greaseproof paper. As soon as the liquid has boiled, add the flour all at once, using the paper as a funnel. Immediately stir really briskly. It should form a ball, and will leave the sides of the pan. Leave to cool just a little, before adding the egg. I find it much easier to add this in a food processor. If you don't have one, beat very well using a wooden spoon.

Beat the eggs — sometimes you may need all the egg, at other times a little may be left. Add the egg a little at a time, and beat well. It needs to be thoroughly blended through or the choux will not stiffen to a paste which holds a shape. At the finish, be a little cautious before adding the last portion of egg. It should be glossy and firm enough to hold a soft peak. It should leave the spoon only with some firm shaking. The procedure is much faster in a food processor, it only takes about 2 minutes.

Mark out a circle about 18 cm (7″) on the baking sheet or, if you have a good eye, you can judge as you pipe. Put the mixture into a piping bag with a plain large nozzle. Pipe out a circle. Do it slowly and try and judge that you have enough for the whole circle.

If there is any egg left, use it to glaze. Otherwise use a little egg yolk mixed with a teaspoon of water, or another egg. Brush over the top of the choux, scatter on the flaked almonds. Place into a moderately hot oven (200°C/400°F) and cook for 15 minutes. Lower the oven temperature to 180°C/350°F and leave to cook a further 10–15 minutes. The pastry should be dry and golden, to pale, brown. If it is colouring too much and you don't think it is quite dry enough, turn the oven off and leave for a further 10 minutes.

Remove and, while warm, carefully cut around the top with a serrated knife and lift off the top to allow it to cool without steaming. When almost cold use a teaspoon to scrape away any uncooked or soft pastry inside.

FILLING

1 cup (8 fl oz) cream

rind of 1 large orange, grated

2 tbsp caster sugar

2 tbsp orange juice

1 tbsp Grand Marnier

1 punnet (250 g/8 oz) strawberries

icing sugar (confectioner's sugar)

Whip the cream until it holds soft peaks. Add the orange rind and sugar and whisk again until stiff. Fold in the orange juice and Grand Marnier. It should be stiff. Hull the berries. Medium-sized ones are best for this dish. If they are large you may need to halve them.

Arrange a layer of cream, just a very thin one in the base of the choux pastry, and then place berries into this. Top with the remainder of the cream and the lid of the choux circle. Dust with some sifted icing sugar and keep chilled.

It will go soft if kept for more than 4–5 hours, so is best assembled as close to dinnertime as possible. Cut into thick slices to serve.

Serves 8–10

LEMON SNOW EGGS WITH ORANGE SAUCE

Tartly refreshing, this is an easy dessert that looks glamorous in presentation. Oval-shaped pale, fragile lemon eggs rest in a pool of translucent orange sauce, with segments of orange between. There is some wastage in assembling this. Little untidy scraps of the lemon mixture remain in the bowl after the eggs are shaped. This amount will only serve four, allowing three 'eggs' per serve. Spooned into dessert dishes, it would be ample for six.

Use a dessertspoon to form the eggs, dipping into warm water and scooping gently around the edge of the bowl. Even if they are not a perfect shape, once assembled this is not noticeable.

3 tsp gelatine
2 tbsp water
1 cup (8 fl oz) water
¾ cup caster sugar
grated rind 1 lemon
⅓ cup lemon juice
2 egg whites
2 tbsp caster sugar
¼ cup (2 fl oz) cream

Mix the gelatine with the 2 tablespoons of water and dissolve in a cup over hot water. Put cup of water into a saucepan with sugar, lemon rind and juice. Bring to a boil. Add the gelatine and chill until slightly jellied. Beat until very frothy.

Beat egg whites until stiff, add the caster sugar, beat again, and fold through the mixture. Then add cream, lightly whipped. Pour into a shallow bowl and chill, if you wish to make egg shapes, or else pour into small individual dishes or into wine glasses. Chill until set. This takes several hours.

ORANGE SAUCE

zest of 1 orange, removed in fine thin strips
1½ cups (12 fl oz) orange juice
3 tbsp sugar

Put the orange strips into a small saucepan, cover with plenty of cold water and bring to a boil. Cook gently for a couple of minutes, and strain. Return them to the pan with orange juice and sugar and cook gently until the rind is tender and the liquid has reduced by half. Cool.

TO SERVE

Form egg shapes with a spoon dipped in warm water. Arrange these on a small puddle of the orange sauce and, if you wish, fan some orange segments around or between the lemon eggs.

VARIATION

When the orange sauce has cooled, add the pulp of 2 passionfruit to it.

Pavlova

Controversy still rages as to whether the first pavlova was made by former shearers' cook Herbert Sachse or whether it was a New Zealand invention.

The story goes that Sachse was working as a chef for Perth's Esplanade Hotel when the licensee asked him to create a tempting dish for afternoon tea. The pavlova is apparently what he came up with, so named because it was 'as light as Pavlova', the leading ballerina of the day.

This is Herbert Sachse's original recipe, which has less sugar than later versions. These often allow for about 1 ½ – 1 ¾ cups of sugar to 6 egg whites.

A perfect pavlova is not white, like meringue, but creamy in colour with a fluffy soft white centre. It needs to be filled at least one hour, preferably several, before eating so it mellows and softens slightly.

6 egg whites
pinch of cream of tartar
few drops vanilla essence
1 rounded cup caster sugar
1 tsp cornflour (cornstarch)
2 bare tsp white vinegar
additional tbsp sugar
additional tbsp cornflour or arrowroot

Beat the egg whites with cream of tartar and vanilla until very firm. Mix the sugar and cornflour together and fold these into the egg whites, being sure to mix them through well, lifting the meringue from the base and folding. Add the vinegar and stir through.

Put a piece of non-stick baking paper on a flat tray. Sift a little of the additional sugar and cornflour or arrowroot in a thin layer on the paper and pile the pavlova directly onto this, smoothing out to make a cake shape. Sprinkle the remainder of the arrowroot and sugar through a sieve over the top.

Have the oven heated to hot (220°C/425°F) and put the pavlova in the centre.

Instantly turn the oven down to low (160°C/300°F) and cook for about 1 ½ hours or until very crisp on the outside. If becoming too brown at any stage you can turn the oven off and leave in the oven. The warmth will continue cooking it.

Remove from the oven and leave to settle about 10 minutes, then turn upside down onto a serving plate so the thicker, crisper portion is now on the base.

Fill with cream or passionfruit curd filling.

PASSIONFRUIT FILLING

3 egg yolks
grated rind 1 lemon
3 tbsp lemon juice
⅓ cup (2½ fl oz) passionfruit pulp
½ cup sugar
60 g (2 oz) unsalted butter, chopped into small pieces
1 cup (8 fl oz) cream

This makes enough for one pavlova. You can either make this filling in a double boiler, which is slow and tedious, or directly over the heat. This is much faster but you need to watch and whisk constantly. Place the yolks, lemon rind and juice, and passionfruit pulp with sugar, either into a double boiler or a small saucepan, and whisk to blend them. Cook, whisking constantly until lightly thickened. Lift the pan off the heat if it is thickening too fast and cooking on the base. (If you are using a double boiler, you only need to stir occasionally. Once it becomes warm watch a bit more carefully.)

When the mixture has lightly thickened — it will barely coat a spoon — add the butter, about a third at a time, whisking until it melts. You can return to the heat, but you won't need it to cook much as the warmth of the mixture should melt it easily. When all the butter has been added, leave to cool in a bowl.

Refrigerate. Covered, you can store it for about 10 days. Stir before using.

Whip the cream until it holds stiff peaks and stir in the passionfruit curd until thoroughly blended through. Spread over the top of the pavlova and leave to rest for the flavours to blend a little with the meringue for about 1 hour. It can be left for up to 12 hours.

CHRISTMAS FLUFF

Although this recipe involves a fairly lengthy preparation, the mince fruit filling keeps beautifully for several weeks, and the basic sponge cake freezes very successfully. When assembled and left for a day or so the flavours blend and the cake softens. It has a light, fluffy taste, and almost melts in your mouth. Because of the minced fruit, I often use this around the festive season. It is a lovely party dish and has the advantage that you can prepare most of it in advance.

FRUIT MINCE

grated rind 1 orange
½ cup (4 fl oz) orange juice
1 small apple, peeled, cored and diced into very tiny pieces
1 small pear, peeled, cored and diced very small
⅓ cup sultanas
1 tbsp glacé cherries, diced
4 dried apricots, diced
1 tbsp mixed peel
2 tbsp brown sugar
2 tbsp brandy

Place everything into a saucepan, except the brandy, and cook very gently (covered) for about 15–20 minutes, or until the apple and pear are quite soft. If very wet, remove the lid and boil rapidly until there is only a little moisture around the fruit. Watch as it can catch on the base.

Remove to a bowl, add the brandy and leave at least 12 hours before using. Keep in a sealed container in the refrigerator, if storing.

CAKE

This mixture makes two cakes, but you need only one for the dessert. It is difficult to prepare half of the mixture, so make the full quantity and freeze the second cake. It keeps well for 6 weeks and can be used directly from the freezer. The texture is of a light, very moist sponge cake.

3 eggs, separated
½ cup sugar
⅓ cup cornflour (cornstarch)
2 tbsp flour
1 tsp baking powder
1 tsp vanilla essence

Butter two round or square tins, 20 cm (8″) in size, and line the base with buttered greaseproof paper.

Beat the egg whites until stiff. Add the sugar, a little at a time, beating until a stiff meringue. Add the yolks one at a time and mix through.

Sift the cornflour, flour and baking powder with a pinch of salt over the top. Fold gently, but be sure there are no flour patches. Flavour with vanilla.

Pour into the prepared tins and bake until it is firm to touch and has come away slightly from the sides. This mixture makes two very thin cakes, but this is the depth needed for this dessert. If you wanted to make this as a light sponge to fill with cream and then ice, for morning or

Lemon Snow Eggs (page 80).

Two Perfumed Fruit Tarts (page 54): a berry tart and a peach tart.

afternoon teas, you would make it in one deep tin, 23 cm (9″) in size. It would then be a much higher cake.

Bake in a moderate oven (180°C/350°F) for about 15–18 minutes for the thin cakes for this dessert. Allow about 25 minutes if you are making one larger cake.

Once you prepare the filling for this dessert you need to assemble immediately or the fluffy texture flattens.

LEMON FILLING

1 tbsp gelatine
¼ cup (2 fl oz) lemon juice
3 eggs
½ cup caster sugar
1½ cups (12 fl oz) milk
grated rind 1 lemon

Mix the gelatine and lemon juice together, then warm in a cup standing in a pan of hot water until dissolved. Separate the eggs, beat the yolks with sugar until thick and fluffy. Heat the milk with lemon rind and add to the yolks, whisking constantly. Return to the heat and cook as for a custard. You can use a whisk with a circular motion; the filling should be fluffy on top. Be careful not to let it boil. Remove from the heat and add the gelatine.

Beat the whites until very stiff and gradually add the hot custard, folding gently but thoroughly. It will have a very fluffy texture.

TO ASSEMBLE

Use the same sized cake tin as the one in which the cake was made. No need to line it as the dessert can be easily turned out. Pour barely half of the lemon filling into the tin and put into the refrigerator or freezer until set. Leave the remainder out so it will stay soft. When becoming firm, carefully cover with a layer of the mince, dotting it here and there on top and then spreading out with a fork. Retain a spoonful for decoration, if you wish.

Stir the remaining half of the lemon filling — it will have subsided quite a bit — and pour over the top. Return to the refrigerator to firm. Cut the sponge in half, horizontally. It is very thin so use a serrated knife. If a fresh sponge, freeze for 30 minutes to make this easier.

Place half the cake, cut side down, on the filling and return to the refrigerator to firm. Once set firmly, dip the tin into warm water to loosen, and turn out onto a serving plate. Place the second half of the cake, cut side down, on the top. If not creaming within a few hours, cover with plastic wrap and return to the refrigerator. It can be left 48 hours at this stage. Once creamed, serve within 12 hours.

TO FINISH

1 cup cream, lightly whipped

spoonful of fruit mince (if you kept this aside) or a few slivers of angelica or pieces of dried or glacé apricot

Cover the top and sides of the cake with cream. Pipe a row of rosettes on the base and around the top. In the centre make a small circle of cream, using a piping bag, and fill this with the fruit mince. If you use angelica you can pipe a rosette in the centre and place some thin fine strips of angelica to radiate out of this in a pattern, or perhaps make a petal pattern with apricot and angelica. The filling will be wider than the sponge, which always shrinks slightly during baking. You can leave it as it is or trim it level. Either way it looks attractive.

Return to the refrigerator. There is no way you can cover this without ruining the decorations (unless you have a huge cake tin), so be sure there is nothing in the refrigerator which may taint the cream.

Serves 10

MERINGUE LEMON CAKE

It may seem a lot of a bother to make this dessert cake, but it can be baked weeks before and frozen. The lemon-butter is tart, the cake light and spongy, and a soft meringue provides a fluffy sweetness around the outside. It looks pretty topped with berries or vivid green kiwi fruit.

LEMON-BUTTER

60 g (2 oz) butter
½ cup sugar
3 egg yolks
grated rind 1 lemon
¼ cup (2 fl oz) lemon juice
additional 30 g (1 oz) unsalted butter

Place all the ingredients, except the additional 30 g (1 oz) of unsalted butter, into a saucepan and stir or whisk well.

Cook over low heat, constantly stirring or beating with a whisk until it is thickened. The mixture must not be allowed to become so hot it boils. If you can't watch it all the time, cook it in a basin over a saucepan of simmering water, giving just an occasional stir. It does take ages, however, if done this way.

Once ready, leave to cool, giving it an occasional stir, then refrigerate, covered. It keeps about 2 weeks.

CAKE

2 eggs
⅓ cup caster sugar
3 tbsp cornflour (cornstarch)
1 tbsp flour
¾ tsp baking powder
pinch salt

Grease a sponge or cake tin 20 cm (8″) and line the base with non-stick paper.

Separate the eggs and beat the whites until stiff. Gradually add the sugar and beat again. Mix in the yolks, one at a time, and stir.

Sift the cornflour, flour and baking powder with salt over the top and fold through gently, but be sure there are no traces of dry ingredients.

Pour into the prepared tin and bake in a moderate oven (180°C/ 350°F) for 18–20 minutes, until firm to touch in the centre, and golden to light brown in colour. It will usually shrink away from the sides slightly when cooked. Remove and leave for 5 minutes before turning out onto a cake rack. Leave to cool and store in a cake tin if not using that day. The basic cake freezes well. There's no need to let it thaw before assembling.

TO ASSEMBLE

3 egg whites
6 tbsp caster sugar
1 punnet (250 g/8 oz) strawberries, raspberries or a mixture of various berries

Ideally, you need to assemble the dessert on a heat-proof plate, because it will go into the oven. If you don't have one you could cover a plate with a double thickness of foil; this should effectively protect the plate for the short time it will be in the oven.

Split the cake in halves and spread one with half of the lemon butter. Place the other layer of cake on this and spread the top with the remainder of the lemon.

Beat the egg whites until stiff and gradually add the sugar, beating until glossy. Spread it over the top and sides of the cake. You can pipe an edge if you wish, although it is just as effective to form a little edge with the back of a spoon.

Place the meringue-covered cake into a moderately hot oven (200°C/400°F) for about 10 minutes or until the meringue is set to touch and golden to light brown in colour.

Cool before serving. Leave 8 hours before cutting to mellow, although it keeps well for 24 hours. Fill the centre with some berries just before you take the cake to the table. Don't sugar them, there is quite enough sweetness in the meringue.

Serves 8

Hot Puddings

In early times puddings were packed into animal guts for boiling. No doubt these would have been carefully cleaned, but the thought is most unattractive. For a long time a hot pudding was known as a 'pudding pye' because a topping of pastry was often laid over a pudding mixture to retain moisture while it was cooked. When, in the 17th century, a cloth was discovered to be ideal for boiling a pudding many more cooks became interested in hot puddings.

Most people, today, are health-conscious and prefer to eat lightly after a main course. So none of these puddings are heavy — apart from a Christmas pudding which has kept its traditional richness; Christmas being the one time of year when nobody seems to worry about their diet.

Most of these puddings need to be served when they are made, because they become heavier when reheated, except, of course, crepe desserts which take very well to reheating.

Further recipes for traditional hot desserts may be found in Old-Fashioned Puddings on page 100.

BASIC CREPES

½ cup flour
pinch salt
2 eggs
½–¾ cup (4–6 fl oz) milk
1 tbsp flavourless oil, or
1 tbsp melted butter
additional butter to cook the crepes

Sift the flour with pinch of salt into a bowl. Make a well in the centre and add the eggs. Stir the eggs with a whisk to break them up and then gradually whisk in the flour from the outside, adding a little milk if it becomes too firm. Gradually add the remainder of the milk, stirring with the whisk. Then mix in the oil or butter. Don't over-mix a crepe batter or it needs to rest for a longer time — the resting period gives it lightness. There should not be any lumps; whisk if there are and, if for any reason, it is still not smooth you can always pour it through a strainer.

Leave standing at room temperature for 30 minutes. It will thicken slightly, and you may need to add a few more spoonfuls of milk. The batter should be like a light cream. The first crepe you make gives a good indication as to whether the texture is right. If it's not, you can add more spoonfuls of milk if necessary.

Heat a crepe pan, I use one which is 14 cm (5½"). This quantity of batter will give you 14 crepes, but sometimes the first one is not good enough to serve, so allow for a discard or two.

When the pan is hot add a tiny piece of butter, about the size of half a walnut for the first, then you will find you need a little less for the remainder. Tilt the pan to coat with butter — it should be sizzling hot — and tip away any excess. Pour in enough batter to coat the pan.
If there is any excess, tip away. (Although tiny, these crepes look attractive, and are easy to handle. If you prefer larger ones, increase the quantity of batter.)

Cook over fairly high heat until set on top. Lift the edge and turn over and cook on the second side which will cook much faster. As each one is done, pile them on top of one another and cover with foil until needed.

Refrigerate them. They can be left 6 hours, but if leaving longer than this it is best to store them with some plastic wrap between each cooled crepe, so they don't stick together. You can then leave 24 hours.

CREPES WITH CARAMEL SAUCE

A quick easy way to cook a buttery orange sauce over crepes by heating under the griller until caramelised. Orange juice freshens the taste, as well as preventing the crepes drying too much.

12 basic crepes

SAUCE

60 g (2 oz) unsalted butter
½ tsp ground cinnamon
grated rind 1 orange
½ cup brown sugar
1 tbsp rum
½ cup (4 fl oz) orange juice
an additional tbsp rum (or more if you like)

Fold each crepe in half, then fold over again (into quarters). Place them in one layer in a shallow ovenproof dish which fits under the griller (broiler).

Cream the butter with cinnamon and orange rind, add sugar and, when fluffy, add the rum a little at a time. This butter can be prepared the day before if you wish.

When you are ready to cook the crepes squeeze the orange juice over them so they are moistened. Dot the top of each one with tiny bits of the butter and place under a preheated griller until the butter is bubbling and lightly caramelised. Watch the crepes; they shouldn't become too crisp on the edges. The orange juice will protect them from drying but if they are browning too much, stop cooking.

Warm the additional rum and ignite. Pour over the crepes and serve immediately.

Serves 4

RUM CREPES

The rum flavour in these crepes is mild but interesting, even when they are served quite simply with lemon wedges and a scatter of fine sugar. They are also very successful served with caramel sauce or with hot, sugary sautéed bananas.

½ cup flour
pinch salt
2 large eggs
2 tbsp brown rum
½ – ¾ cup (4–6 fl oz) milk
2 tsp light flavoured oil, or
2 tsp unsalted butter

Sift the flour and salt into a bowl. Make a well in the centre and add the eggs. Break them up with a whisk and add the rum. Whisk, gradually incorporating the flour from the sides, adding a little milk if it becomes at all dry. Then whisk in the remaining milk and blend with the whisk until smooth. Don't overbeat; the crepes will need to stand longer if you do.

Lastly, add oil or butter and leave the mixture at room temperature for 30 minutes or until it has thickened slightly. If too thick add a spoonful or two of milk, or wait until you cook the first crepe, and judge by its thickness whether or not to add milk. (The first crepe is rarely perfect.)

Make up as for basic crepes. This quantity of batter will give you 14 crepes, allowing for a couple of discards.

Serves 4

A VERY LIGHT ORANGE AND WALNUT PUDDING

A divinely light pudding, moist with orange and syrup, which is poured over the top once it has been steamed. Lovely with thick pouring cream or vanilla ice-cream alongside.

½ cup brown sugar
⅓ cup (2½ fl oz) orange juice
90 g (3 oz) butter
grated rind of 1 large or 2 medium-sized oranges
2 eggs
1 cup breadcrumbs, made from stale white bread
2 tbsp finely chopped walnuts

Butter a basin which you can place into a saucepan, either a steam pudding basin or a china one is best. It should hold about 3 cups.

Heat the sugar and orange juice gently in a saucepan, boil until syrupy, then leave to cool. You should have a bare ½ cup of syrup.

Cream the butter with orange rind until light. Separate the eggs. Add the yolks, one at a time, to the butter. Mix in breadcrumbs.

Pour in the cooled syrup and beat; it will become quite a thick mixture. Mix through walnuts and, lastly, egg whites, beaten until stiff. Add just a little first to lighten the mixture, as it is quite thick, then add the remainder. Place into the pudding basin, cover with either a lid, if a steam pudding basin, or two thicknesses of foil, firmly tied.

Steam with water to come about one third of the way up the sides, for 1 hour.

SAUCE

½ cup (4 fl oz) orange juice
1 tbsp brown sugar
1 tbsp Grand Marnier

While the pudding is cooking prepare the sauce; it can be warmed again when you are ready to use.

Cook the orange juice gently with the sugar until the sugar has dissolved. Cook until syrupy and leave aside. Add the Grand Marnier just before pouring over the pudding. Invert the pudding onto a plate and spoon the warm sauce over the top. Some will soak into the pudding, a little will run down the sides onto the dish.

Serves 4–6

ZUCCHINI STEAMED PUDDING

Zucchini gives a lovely moist texture to a pudding, just as it does to cake. It looks interesting, with light fine green shreds throughout, and is studded generously with sultanas (golden raisins). If you have any left over, it can be eaten, lightly spread with butter as a tea cake.

¾ cup sultanas

125 g (4 oz) butter

¾ cup light brown sugar

2 large eggs

125 g (4 oz) zucchini

1 cup flour

1 tsp baking powder

½ tsp bicarbonate soda

½ tsp allspice

1 tsp finely grated orange rind

Lightly butter a basin with a 5-cup capacity.

Put the sultanas into a bowl and pour boiling water over them to just cover. Leave standing for 15 minutes, and then drain.

Cream the butter with the brown sugar until light, and add the eggs, one at a time. Grate the zucchini and mix through.

Sift the flour and baking powder with the bicarbonate of soda and spices. Mix half into the creamed mixture and stir well, then add the remainder of the dry ingredients.

Stir through the sultanas and orange rind and mix thoroughly. Spoon into the greased basin, for steaming. Cover with a double thickness of foil and tie firmly around the top.

Put the basin into a large saucepan and add boiling water to come a little more than halfway up the basin. Cook, with the lid on the pan, for 1½ hours, with the water gently bubbling. Check to see it is not boiling away. If it is, top up with a little more boiling water.

Let the pudding rest for 5 minutes before removing the foil and inverting onto a plate. You can serve with some lightly whipped, sweetened cream, or with lemon cream (page 43).

Serves 8

PUFFY CITRUS PUDDING

This was an experiment with an orange soufflé which appeared to be a disaster: the scattered pieces of fresh orange and lemon on top made it collapse. However, we all loved the taste! It is a cross between pudding and soufflé, light and fruity, and even good if served tepid. It won't be as high or so puffed as it cools, but will still taste delicious.

60 g (2 oz) butter
3 tbsp flour
¾ cup (6 fl oz) milk
6 tbsp sugar
grated rind of 1 lemon
grated rind of 1 orange
½ cup (4 fl oz) orange juice
⅓ cup (2½ fl oz) lemon juice
4 eggs
½ orange
½ lemon
icing sugar

Butter an ovenproof dish with a capacity of 5 cups.

Melt the butter and add the flour. Leave to cook gently for a few minutes. Remove from the heat while you add the milk, sugar, lemon and orange rind, orange and lemon juice and stir. Return to the heat and cook, stirring constantly until it comes to the boil and thickens.

Remove from the heat again. Separate the eggs and add the yolks, one at a time. You can prepare this several hours beforehand, but don't refrigerate or it will become too firm.

Remove all the peel and pith from both the orange and lemon halves. Cut the fruit into thin slices, discard any pips and cut into tiny pieces. They must be small so they will flavour the dessert and stay suspended throughout.

Beat the whites until they hold stiff peaks. Fold about one-third at a time into the cooked custard, and pour half into the buttered dish. Scatter the fresh pieces of orange and lemon on top, then spoon over the remainder of the mixture. Bake in a moderate oven (180°C/350°F) for about 25–30 minutes or until just set. It can remain a little creamy in the centre. Dust with sifted icing sugar before serving.

Serves 6

RICH FRUIT PUDDING

125 g (4 oz) sultanas
125 g (4 oz) raisins, cut into halves
60 g (2 oz) glacé cherries
60 g (2 oz) mixed peel
60 g (2 oz) glacé apricots, diced small
30 g (1 oz) glacé ginger, cut into slices
1 tbsp brown rum
60 g (2 oz) blanched almonds, roughly chopped
125 g (4 oz) brown sugar
125 g (4 oz) butter
2 eggs
grated rind of 1 lemon
grated rind of 1 orange
60 g (2 oz) flour
½ tsp mixed spice
½ tsp ground cinnamon
1 medium-sized Granny Smith apple, peeled and grated
1 cup breadcrumbs, made from stale bread

Butter a 6-cup capacity basin lightly and line the base with a circle of non-stick or heavy greaseproof paper. Butter the paper.

Put all the fruit into a large bowl and add the rum, giving it a good stir. Put a plate over the top and leave to stand for 24 hours. Mix in the nuts.

Cream the sugar with butter until fluffy, add the eggs, one at a time, the lemon and orange rind and sift the flour with spices over the top. Stir through fruit mix, and lastly add the apple and crumbs. Give it a really good stir for about a minute with a wooden spoon, and spoon into the mould.

Cover the top with a double thickness of foil tied firmly or, if you use a steam pudding basin, some of these have a clip-on lid. Cook with enough water to come at least halfway up the pudding for 2½ hours.

You can serve it with ice-cream, or a custard sauce. For an even richer flavour serve a hard sauce — the type which is traditionally on the table on Christmas Day — made from butter, icing-sugar, brandy or rum and a little cinnamon. These very buttery hard sauces tend to make the dessert seem sweet, and so are mainly suitable if the remainder of the dinner has been light and fresh.

Serves 8–10

A SIMPLE CHRISTMAS PLUM PUDDING

This pudding is simple, but still very good and moist because of the apple and carrot used in the mixture. It is one which needs only to be made a few days before Christmas — unlike the heavier classic puddings — so is ideal for busy households. It should easily serve 8 people, and can be doubled.

---

250 g (8 oz) packet of mixed fruit
125 g (4 oz) seedless raisins
½ tsp mixed spice
½ tsp cinnamon
90 g (3 oz) soft brown sugar
90 g (3 oz) suet
1 medium-sized carrot, peeled
185 g (6 oz) breadcrumbs made from stale white or wholemeal bread
1 large apple, peeled
1 tbsp orange marmalade
2 large eggs
1 tbsp brandy

Butter a steam-pudding basin — one which holds 10 cups. Put the mixed fruit and raisins into a large mixing bowl, and add spices. Stir through the brown sugar and crumbs. Chop the suet finely and add. Grate both carrot and apple over the top. (There should be about 2 cups of grated mixture.) Mix in the marmalade and give everything a stir.

Beat the eggs lightly, add the brandy and stir into the mixture, mixing with a spoon for about a minute. Put into the well-greased pudding basin and cover the top with a layer of greaseproof paper and then a double thickness of foil. Tie the basin firmly, leaving the ends of the knot hanging so you can use them to help remove the pudding from the saucepan.

Put into a large saucepan, add sufficient boiling water to come about ⅔ of the way up the pudding. Simmer gently with the lid on for about 4½ hours, checking occasionally to see the water is not boiling away. If it needs replenishing, top with more boiling water.

Let the pudding cool and then cover with some fresh greaseproof paper and foil and store in a cool place. On Christmas Day, simmer for another 2½ hours.

Serves 8

A CLASSIC CHRISTMAS PUDDING

Even the most sophisticated food writers talk, not about modern Christmas puddings, but about their mothers' or their grandmothers' puddings or they speak with nostalgia about stirring the pudding for good luck, adding trinkets, threepences and charms.

Traditionally, puddings are made in a cloth. Pudding cloths, usually with clear instructions as to what to do before they are used, are available in some department stores. But a basin is easier. There is less risk of any water seeping into the pudding, and it is good for storing the pudding.

Most recipes use suet, which you can buy in packages, but be careful. Avoid those that have added flour because this throws all the ingredients out of proportion, spoiling the pudding. Far better to buy suet from the butcher and shred it, discarding any membrane or bits with blood. You need to get about double what the recipe says because there is a lot of wastage.

When the magnificent pudding is finally turned out, scatter the top with a little icing sugar and heat some brandy in a small saucepan. Set it alight and take the pudding to the table, the top burning with blue flames. But watch that sprig of holly (if it's on top). Sometimes it can also catch alight.

This pudding is based on a recipe which is more than 100 years old, and appeared in Eliza Acton's *Modern Cookery* (published in London in 1845). It is very large, the type for big family gatherings, but you can halve it if you have only a small number around the dinner table. There is no sugar; the fruits make it quite sweet enough.

125 g (4 oz) glacé cherries, cut into halves
125 g (4 oz) mixed peel
750 g (1½ lb) seedless raisins, cut into halves
125 g (4 oz) blanched almonds
125 g (4 oz) currants
1 tbsp flour
375 g (12 oz) suet, grated
375 g (12 oz) breadcrumbs, made from stale white or wholemeal bread
½ tsp nutmeg
1 tsp cinnamon
½ tsp allspice
8 large eggs
6 tbsp rum or brandy
¼ cup (2 fl oz) beer or stout

Butter a pudding basin which holds 10 cups of mixture. Put all the fruits and nuts into a bowl and add the flour, stirring so it separates the fruit. Mix in crumbs, suet, cinnamon and other spices. Beat the eggs until frothy, add the rum and beer or stout and mix into the dry ingredients. The mixture should drop easily from a spoon. Mix very well, stirring for a minute with a big wooden spoon.

Put into the greased pudding basin, and make a little hollow in the centre so the pudding will be level when cooked.

If you are making one large pudding, it will take 7 hours for the first steaming, but if you divide the mixture into two basins, 5½–6 hours should be long enough.

Cover the pudding with greaseproof paper and then a double thickness of foil. Cook in a large saucepan with boiling water, checking it every so often for topping up with more water. When cooked, cover with fresh foil for storing and keep in a cool place.

On Christmas Day, steam again about 3–3½ hours (or 2½ hours for the smaller puddings).

Serves 16 generously

Serves 8

Old-fashioned Puddings

Traditional, old-fashioned — whatever you like to call them — nostalgic puddings are back in fashion.

In a book I recently read about English clubs and predominantly masculine restaurants, it was recorded that men's tastes in puddings were conservative. The puddings of their childhood remained their favourites, and the older the man the more nostalgic were his tastes.

There are times when everybody feels like the comforting taste of a warm rice pudding, a home-made apple pie or a custard tart, and some classic dishes like summer pudding and crème brûlée have never really gone out of fashion.

In some cases I have modified original recipes to make them a little lighter and more in keeping with modern tastes. These days, most people don't want to end a meal with a dessert that is too rich or heavy.

Pear Mould with a Caramel Ginger Sauce (page 13) and Madeleines (page 128).

Layered Chocolate Mould (page 120)
and White Chocolate Mousses (page 115).

Bread-and-Butter Pudding in the Style of the Dorchester

On a visit to the grill room at the Dorchester Hotel in London I was surprised to see Bread-and-butter Pudding on the menu. 'One of our most popular desserts', the immaculately clad waiter assured me when I ordered a serve.

It bore little resemblance to nursery-type, or boarding house-style of puddings: a soft creamy custard spiked with dried fruits and a crunchy top formed by slicing white dinner rolls instead of bread, so there was a higher proportion of crust.

I love it with running cream and so, it seems, do most people.

2 small long dinner rolls
30 g (1 oz) softened butter
2 tbsp currants
2 tbsp sultanas
1½ cups (12 fl oz) milk
1½ cups (12 fl oz) cream
2 eggs
1 egg yolk
3 tbsp caster sugar
½ tsp vanilla essence

Remove the crusts from the ends of the bread rolls and cut the rolls into medium thin slices. Butter each slice.

Scatter about half the currants and sultanas over the base of a lightly buttered dish, one which has a capacity of about 5 cups.

Place the milk and cream into a saucepan and warm slightly. Whisk or beat the eggs with the egg yolk and sugar until frothy, and gradually pour the hot milk and cream over the top. Add the vanilla essence. Pour this through a sieve onto the top of the bread. Do it as evenly as possible to be sure all the bread is moistened. Scatter the remaining currants and sultanas on top.

Place in a baking tin and add boiling water, to come about halfway up the sides of your dish. Bake in a barely moderate oven (160°C/325°F) for about 40 to 45 minutes, or until it is just set.

Serve it warm, not hot, from the oven. It is best left standing for about 20 minutes.

Serves 6–8

Apple bread-and-butter pudding

A variation on the traditional pudding, the bread is sandwiched with apple and the custard cooked on top, a lighter dish when prepared with fruit. Serve with or without cream; both ways are nice.

500 g (1 lb) cooking apples
30 g (1 oz) butter
2 tbsp sugar
¼ tsp ground cinnamon
3 tbsp water
2 tbsp currants
4 slices wholemeal bread
some butter
2 eggs
1 egg yolk
2 cups (16 fl oz) milk
½ tsp vanilla essence
¼ cup sugar

Peel, core and slice the apples thinly and place into a saucepan with the butter, sugar, cinnamon and water. Stir the apples so they are coated with liquid, cover the pan and cook them gently until soft. Give them an occasional stir. If there is a lot of liquid around the fruit, cook over a high heat for a few minutes until it has reduced to a thick syrup. Make sure it doesn't burn on the base. Add the currants while the apple is warm and mix through.

Spread each slice of bread with butter and cut into four squares. Place a layer of bread, the buttered side up, on the base of a shallow ovenproof dish. Use one which has a capacity of about 5 cups, and approximately 25 cm x 18 cm (9½″ x 7″) in diameter. Spread the cooked apples over the top and then place the remaining bread over this, buttered side up.

Beat the eggs with milk and vanilla, sugar, and whisk well. Pour through a sieve over the top of the bread, making sure you moisten each piece. Place the dish in a baking try which has enough hot water to come about halfway up the side of the dish.

Bake in a moderate oven (180°C/350°F) for about 30 minutes, or until set on top. (It will firm a little more as it rests.) Remove before it puffs up in the centre; this usually means it is over-cooked. Leave to set for 10 minutes before serving.

You can dust the top with a sprinkle of cinnamon if you wish, or scatter on some caster sugar, although it is really quite flavoured and sweet enough to be left as it is.

Serves 4

Spanish cream

This dessert separates into layers: the base with the passionfruit has an almost clear jellied appearance, the centre is creamy, and the top is frothy. This is a very light dessert, with enough gelatine to set it, but only lightly. It can't be unmoulded. So place into individual dishes or glasses, preferably clear ones, so the effect of the layers can be seen.

3 cups (24 fl oz) milk
2 egg yolks
3 tbsp sugar
1 tbsp and 1 tsp gelatine
3 tbsp water
½ tsp vanilla essence
4 large passionfruit
2 egg whites

Heat the milk. While it is warming, beat the egg yolks with sugar in a basin and add the hot milk gradually, constantly stirring. Return to the saucepan and cook, stirring with a whisk until lightly thickened. Don't let it boil, and don't expect it to be like a thick custard. It will be very light.

Mix the gelatine with water, stir and add to the hot custard. It should dissolve easily. Leave the custard to cool completely. Flavour with vanilla and the pulp of the 4 passionfruit. When the dessert is completely cold, but not yet set, beat the egg whites until they hold stiff peaks. Fold them through, one third at a time, and pour into a dessert bowl or small individual dishes. Chill until set. It usually takes about 4 hours to firm.

Serves 6–8

SUMMER PUDDING

'Be sure to use good bread' are the first words in most of the best recipes for this famous English pudding. This means avoid the soft white sliced commercial bread which absorbs the berry juices but becomes the texture of blotting paper in your mouth. One-day-old 'country-styled bread' with a slightly coarser texture is the best.

The strawberries must always be fresh (not frozen) or they are horrible and soggy. If they aren't available you could substitute loganberries or youngberries. The raspberries must also be fresh or the flavour is reduced.

Regardless of how well-known this dessert is, it is still extraordinarily popular, enjoyed with a jug of thick rich cream, rather than whipped cream.

---

2 tsp gelatine
1 tbsp water
250 g (8 oz) raspberries
¼ cup sugar
¼ cup (2 fl oz) water
125 g (4 oz) small strawberries or halved large berries
250 g (8 oz) blackberries
½ cup (4 fl oz) water
¼ cup sugar
1 loaf one-day-old white bread

Mix the gelatine and tablespoon of water together.

Place the raspberries into a saucepan with the sugar and ¼ cup of water and bring to the boil. Remove from the heat immediately. Add half the gelatine, stir gently and leave to cool. Add the strawberries.

Place the blackberries into a saucepan with ½ cup of water and the sugar and bring to a boil. Remove and add the remaining gelatine and leave to cool.

Line a mould, which holds about 5 cups, with slices of bread, crusts removed, and cut into triangles. Be sure they fit snugly. Reserve some bread for the centre layer and for the top of the pudding. It doesn't matter if you have to patch the top with left-over bits of bread because it will become the base, and won't be seen.

Place the raspberries and strawberries into a sieve standing over a bowl and leave the juices to drain. Do the same with the blackberries over another bowl. Be careful not to crush the fruit.

Place the raspberry mixture into the bread-lined mould, and then top with another layer of bread, pressing down gently but firmly. Place the blackberries on top of this and arrange more bread on top to completely cover. Mix both the juices together and pour over bread until it appears well soaked. You will probably have some over. Let the pudding rest for about 10 minutes and then add a little more syrup. It should look very wet but not be swimming with so much liquid that it won't soak in.

Place a plate or saucer on top and then a weight, such as a tin. Refrigerate for 12 hours.

Remove the weight and the saucer or plate the next day. Turn this out on a serving plate with a rim (to retain sauce). Invert the dish. The bread should be soaked to a lovely crimson colour. Sometimes it is not evenly soaked but this doesn't matter. Spoon a little of the reserved liquid over the top so it is very moist and sitting in a small pool of juice.

Once you have turned it out, serve the same day.

It would keep well for 48 hours before turning out. Leave it in the refrigerator but remove the weight, leaving the saucer or plate on top.

Serve with cream. It looks prettier decorated with some fresh fruits and mint leaves which have been lightly frosted with icing-sugar.

Serves 6–8

RICE PUDDING

Today, savoury rice dishes, like risotto, are so popular that it seems strange that rice pudding is so rarely made. Is it because the stodgy rice pudding of yesteryear was so often such a cheap nasty affair that the memory lingers? Rice pudding can be exotic, generously filled with fruits and brandy, fresh with orange peel and either creamy or lighter with milk. In Georgian times, the English first put a rim of elaborately decorated pastry around the pudding dish, baked it, and then filled it with the pudding.

¼ cup short grain rice
2 cups (16 fl oz) milk
2 tbsp sugar
2 tbsp sultanas (golden raisins)
1 tbsp chopped mixed dried peel
generous pinch nutmeg
¼ tsp cinnamon
pinch cloves
½ tsp vanilla essence

Everything can be mixed together in the ovenproof dish in which you cook the pudding. You will need one which holds about 4 cups (32 fl oz), and which is not too shallow.

Stir the mixture so the spices, sultanas, etc., are evenly distributed, and place into a moderately slow oven (160°C/ 325°F) and leave for about 90 minutes to 2 hours.

Don't break the skin which forms on top; this is like a seal which prevents the milk from boiling away too quickly. At the end of this time the rice should be tender. Take out a tiny portion to check and taste. You may find there is still liquid around the rice. While it is cooling, the rice will absorb more, and the dish will thicken. Leave 20 minutes before serving. It will keep warmer if you cover loosely with foil.
Serves 4

LEMON MERINGUE PIE

This was always a childhood favourite of mine. My grandmother used to make it, and then my mother carried on the tradition for family Sunday lunches. After a hot roast dinner of beef or lamb the adults would be offered trifle, but the children were forbidden this dessert because the base, layers of jam roll, was saturated with sherry taken from the decanter on the sideboard.

Instead, we were offered lemon meringue pie, which we preferred anyway, with its slightly cakey yet crisp base, a tart filling made from the lemons gathered from the trees in the yard and a thick fluffy meringue on top. There was always lashings of cream — yellow and almost too thick to pour — spooned in a heap alongside.

Sometimes the filling was made with a cornflour base. At other times it was made with condensed milk, which I find rather too firm. I prefer a soft, almost lemon-custard, texture to give a creamy filling on the biscuit base. It is important to use sharp, acid lemons or the meringue tastes too sweet and out of balance.

PIE CRUST

1½ cups self-raising flour
3 tbsp cornflour (cornstarch)
90 g (3 oz) butter
3 tbsp sugar
1 egg yolk
approximately 3 tbsp milk

Sift the flour with the cornflour. Cream the butter and sugar until well-blended and mix in the flour and egg yolk. You can do this by hand or in a food processor. Add sufficient milk so the pastry binds together when pressed between thumb and forefinger. It must hold well but not be too sticky.

Roll out between some waxed paper and place in a shallow pie dish, 23 cm (9″) in diameter. Prick well with a fork and line the top with some non-stick baking paper, pressing down onto the crust.

Bake for 20 minutes in a moderate oven (180°C/350°F). Remove the paper and cook a further 5 minutes, or until a good golden-to-light-brown colour.

Leave to cool before placing the filling in the crust.

FILLING

½ cup (4 fl oz) orange juice
½ cup (4 fl oz) lemon juice
grated rind of 2 lemons
½ cup sugar
3 tbsp cornflour (cornstarch)
3 egg yolks
15 g (½ oz) butter

Mix the juices with lemon rind and sugar in a saucepan. Warm until the sugar has dissolved. Mix a little water with the cornflour in a bowl, add some of the warm juice to this, return to the saucepan and cook until thickened.

Beat the egg yolks to break them up and add, one at a time, to the hot filling, whisking well. Remove from the heat and add the butter and whisk in well. Leave to cool and pour into the pastry case.

MERINGUE

3 egg whites
pinch salt
4 tbsp sugar

Beat the whites with salt until stiff. Add the sugar gradually and beat until very stiff and glossy. Spread over the filling, taking it right to the edges until it covers the lemon completely.

Bake in a moderately slow oven (160°C/325°F) for about 20 minutes. When ready it should be firm to the touch and a pale brown. It will never be even, but the little swirls of movement when you spread on the meringue will have colour variations which add to the interesting appearance.

Serves 8–10

Custard tart

This was once known as a transparent pudding or a sweet egg pie, and has been popular since Elizabethan days.

It is nicest when the crust is quite sweet, more like a biscuit than a pastry; and it is really best baked in a metal container. China pie dishes don't give enough heat to cook the crust through. You can even use a 23 cm (9″) cake tin. This will make it a little difficult to remove the tart, but once one slice is cut the remainder can be taken out more easily. Should you have only glass or china pie plates, cook the crust first, lined with buttered foil to hold up the sides. When set, remove the foil and continue cooking until a pale golden colour.

PASTRY

1 cup flour
½ tsp baking powder
90 g (3 oz) butter
¼ cup caster sugar
1 egg yolk

It can be made in a food processor or by hand. Sift the flour with the baking powder and add the butter. Then process or crumble until in tiny pieces. Mix in the sugar and egg yolk and work to a paste. Knead for 30 seconds. Roll into a ball and let it rest for 20 minutes. If it is very sticky, chill.

Roll out, it's best to do this between greaseproof waxed paper, and line the base and sides of a lightly buttered pie tin with the pastry.

Chill while preparing the filling, or bake blind if you are using a china dish.

FILLING

1½ cups (12 fl oz) milk
½ cup (4 fl oz) cream
2 tbsp sugar
4 eggs
1 tsp vanilla essence

Warm the milk and cream together in a saucepan.

Beat the eggs with sugar and add the warm milk, stirring well. Flavour with vanilla and leave to cool.

Pour the filling into the pastry case and bake in a moderate oven

(180°C/350°F) for 40–45 minutes, or until the custard is set in the centre.

You can leave it plain or dust the top with a little nutmeg if you wish.

Leave to cool, but don't refrigerate. It's best eaten at room temperature within 24 hours of baking.

If you bake the pastry blind, the second stage of setting the custard usually takes about 25–30 minutes.

Serves 8

BUTTERMILK PUDDING

Cleopatra loved buttermilk, according to legend. But she didn't drink it, she used it as a daily beauty mask to keep her skin fresh and glowing. Apart from its uses in the boudoir, buttermilk gives a lightness to batters and cakes. The flavour is slightly tangy and tart due to a culture which has been added. Despite sweetening, this fresh tang still comes through in the pudding; the texture is velvety smooth. Very good on its own, it's even better with sliced fresh peaches, or berries, or accompanied by plain biscuits: little shortbread ones or almond wafers (page 129).

1¼ cups (10 fl oz) buttermilk
½ vanilla bean
3 tsp gelatine
⅓ cup (2½ fl oz) water
⅓ cup caster sugar
¼ cup (2 fl oz) cream
an additional ¼ cup (2 fl oz) cream, lightly whipped

Split the vanilla bean lengthwise and place in a saucepan with the caster sugar and cream. Heat gently and then turn off the heat and leave the bean to steep for 30 minutes, to flavour the mixture. Remove and scrape out the soft black centre and mix through.

Mix the gelatine with the water. Add this to the cream, leave to cool completely and then stir in the buttermilk. It will thicken almost immediately. As soon as it is like a soft jelly, fold in the remaining lightly whipped cream and pour into individual dessert dishes.

Refrigerate until set. Cover if keeping longer than 12 hours. You can prepare this dish 48 hours beforehand if you wish.

Serves 4

Sago plum pudding

Sometimes called Boston pudding, this is much lighter than the usual plum pudding. The sago gives it a translucent appearance and moist texture, making it a good substitute for the standard fruit pudding.

You need to begin the preparation some time beforehand, because the sago has to be soaked to soften it. Apart from this, the preparation is quite fast.

¾ cup sago
1 cup (8 fl oz) milk
1 cup breadcrumbs made from stale white or wholemeal bread
2 tbsp flour
¾ cup sultanas
¼ cup currants
1 tbsp chopped mixed peel
2 tbsp chopped glacé cherries
2 tsp chopped glacé ginger
½ tsp cinnamon
½ tsp mixed spice
60 g (2 oz) butter
1 large egg
¾ cup firmly-packed soft brown sugar
2 tsp bicarbonate soda
2 tbsp boiling water

Grease a pudding basin with a capacity of 5 cups. Put the sago into a bowl and add the milk. Leave to stand for 12 hours, refrigerated.

Mix in the breadcrumbs, flour and fruit with the spices. Melt the butter and add with the egg and sugar. Stir very well.

Dissolve the bicarbonate of soda in the boiling water and mix in last.

Tip the mixture into the basin and fold a double thickness of foil over the top. Tie it firmly in place with string.

Put into a saucepan and add boiling water so it comes about halfway up the sides of the basin. Cook for 2½ hours, checking the water occasionally to make sure it has not boiled away. If you need to replenish it, do this with boiling, not cold, water.

Remove the pudding. Let it sit for 5 minutes before removing the string and turning it out.

Plain cream, brandy, vanilla custard, or hard sauce — they all go well, so you can take your pick. If you want to make up the pudding beforehand, mix all the ingredients, cover the bowl, and refrigerate until ready to cook. It can be left 12 hours at this stage.

Serves 8

Raspberry and Champagne Syllabub

Back in the early 17th century, the mistress of the house would have walked out to the cowshed carrying a deep container called a syllabub pot. In the bottom was a mixture made of sugar with lemon rind and juice, port, madeira or, perhaps, sherry. Milk from the waiting cow was squirted into this so it foamed and frothed to the top. Left to cool in the stillroom, this highly alcoholic dessert, looking innocently frothy, was offered at lunches, dinners, balls and card parties.

Circumstances have changed. The syllabub is now made with cream, and the alcohol content is not as high. It is usually in the form of wine or brandy. A tart fruit, such as lemon, is still usually added.

This version is not at all traditional. The raspberries mixed with champagne give a soft fragile pink colour and lovely, fresh flavour. It's easy to make and even nicer poured over some additional fresh berries, either more raspberries or some strawberries.

125 g (4 oz) fresh or frozen raspberries
½ cup caster sugar
½ cup (4 fl oz) champagne
1 tbsp kirsch
1 cup (8 fl oz) cream
additional raspberries for decorating or serving with the dessert

Push the raspberries through a sieve. You can't blend or process them as the pulp will be too full of pips. Mix with the sugar, champagne and kirsch. Leave to stand about 30 minutes for the sugar to dissolve, or at least soften. Whip the cream until it holds soft peaks, and then gradually add to the cream, whisking so it remains fairly stiff. It will firm more as it is chilled.

Refrigerate, either in individual bowls or a large dish. Leave at least 2 hours before serving, so the flavours will mellow.

Don't decorate with cream. It would be just too creamy, but some fresh berries and a green leaf look very pretty.

Serves 4

CREME BRULEE

Crème Brûleé (burnt cream) has been recorded in England since the 17th century. After almost being forgotten it became popular again when a chef at Trinity College began to make it at the end of the last century. Consisting of eggs, cream and sugar, crème brûleé is not exactly diet food, but if you intend to indulge occasionally, this is a dessert to make it worthwhile. Only a small serve is necessary, and it is usually accompanied by fruit.

I find a strong hot griller essential. It's much easier for a chef to make this dish as he will have a salamander which becomes fiery hot and caramelises almost instantly without heating the custard underneath.

It is topped by brown sugar, or a layer of caster sugar, please yourself which. Brown is more caramel-tasting, and usually melts more quickly. Always watch as the sugar melts. You may need to turn the tray around if the heat is uneven. The sugar should melt and bubble to a marbled golden glassiness. If the custard shows signs of overheating, and boils under the sugar, remove the dish immediately. I haven't had this happen, and it is only likely to under a poor grilling heat, which takes some time.

½ vanilla bean
3 egg yolks
2 tbsp caster sugar or brown sugar
1 cup (8 fl oz) milk
1 cup (8 fl oz) thick cream
¼ cup additional caster sugar or light brown sugar

Cut the vanilla bean in halves lengthwise and, with a small knife, scrape out the soft black section. Place into a bowl and add the yolks, sugar, milk and cream. Whisk together for a few seconds.

Pour into four small individual ovenproof dishes which hold about ¾ cup, or into gratin dishes. Bake in a slow oven (140°C/300°F), or in dishes placed in baking tray of water which comes halfway up, until barely set. The custards should tremble a little in the centre when gently shaken.

Cool slightly and then refrigerate until cold.

Just before dinner sieve the remaining sugar over the top. To protect the edge of your dishes you can place a strip of foil around each one and press to hold it firmly in place. (This can only be done on individual casseroles, such as baby soufflé dishes, not on gratin dishes.)

Place under a very hot griller (broiler) until glazed on top, and a light brown colour. Chill another 15 minutes and then serve.

Serves 4

CHOCOLATE PUDDINGS

A special word has been coined for people who adore chocolate: 'chocoholics'. In America they are in such numbers that there is a magazine devoted solely to the pleasures of eating chocolate.

Theobrome is Greek for 'the food of the gods' and is also the name for the cocoa tree. The Aztecs believed chocolate came from a divine source. They also considered it an aphrodisiac, and the last Aztec ruler, Montezuma always drank a large goblet filled to the brim with frothy chocolate before entering his harem.

The distinct and definite flavour of chocolate can vary in sweetness and richness but in puddings, soufflés, cakes or desserts it is a universal favourite.

When using cocoa to give a chocolate flavour in desserts, always sift it or tiny lumps can remain unevenly throughout.

When melting chocolate, the main rule is always to melt it gently over low heat. If overheated it will form a sticky mass, and the chocolate is said to 'tighten'. Large or uneven pieces will not melt evenly so cut chocolate into small, even pieces before placing in a bowl. Stand this over a saucepan of hot water, making sure the base of the bowl does not touch the water. Leave to warm until melted, then stir, but only gently, until smooth. Don't use a wooden spoon as this can retain strong food flavours if it has been previously used to stir soups or sautéed food.

Chocolate can also be melted in a microwave. Put it onto a suitable plate, or else in a bowl or cup. Cover with plastic wrap and, for timing, follow the directions for your particular microwave.

If you have any chocolate over, it can be most successfully remelted and perhaps used for decorations. Store in the refrigerator, wrapping in a piece of plastic wrap once it is firming. The chocolate which was used to test these particular recipes was semi-sweet.

CREMA DE CHOCOLATE

After its discovery in Mexico, chocolate was brought to Spain. Although we always think of chocolate mousse as a French creation, it originated in Spain. This is the Spanish version. It is like a chocolate mousse but seems lighter in texture than French recipes, although it is still luscious and rich.

90 g (3 oz) dark sweet chocolate
90 g (3 oz) milk sweet chocolate
¼ cup (2 fl oz) strong black coffee
1 tbsp brandy
4 eggs,
¾ cup (6 fl oz) thick cream

Break both the chocolates into squares and put into a bowl. Melt gently, standing the bowl over a saucepan of simmering water. Stir in the coffee and brandy. Separate the eggs and mix in the egg yolks one at a time. The mixture should stiffen and become glossy.

Beat the whites until stiff and beat the cream until it holds stiff peaks. Mix both the whites and cream together and then fold them about a third at a time into the chocolate mixture.

Pour into wine glasses or individual dishes. Refrigerate for 12 hours before eating so it will become slightly firmer. It keeps well for several days, covered with some plastic wrap.
Serves 8

TRADITIONAL CHOCOLATE MOUSSE

French recipes for chocolate mousse always include butter; the more butter the firmer the texture will be. I prefer mousses on the light side, so I use only a little butter. This dessert can be eaten the day it is made, but improves if you leave to mature for 24 hours.

185 g (6 oz) dark semi-sweet chocolate
30 g (1 oz) unsalted butter
1 tbsp rum, brandy or orange-flavoured liqueur
3 eggs

Break the chocolate into pieces. Put into a bowl or the top of a double boiler with the butter and leave to melt over hot water. Stir gently until smooth, and add rum, brandy or liqueur.

Separate the eggs and add the yolks, one at a time, mixing thoroughly or whisking. The mixture should be very smooth and glossy. Beat the whites until stiff. Add one-third to the chocolate, then fold in the remainder. You should fold gently but thoroughly enough so no portion of white remains.

Pour into small mousse containers or tiny dishes. It is very rich so should make 6 portions.

Refrigerate at least 5–6 hours. It's best if left 24 hours for the mousse to thicken and mellow.

A rosette of whipped cream, while adding to the richness, looks pretty on top, and a small frosted or candied flower such as a violet adds to the effect.

Serves 6

WHITE CHOCOLATE MOUSSE

Although made in a similar manner to milk or dark chocolate, white chocolate contains cocoa butter instead of chocolate liqueur, and is not considered true chocolate. It makes a very sweet mousse so it is best served in small portions. Apart from the fine decorative piping on top, you can add a candied violet or neaten the edges with rosettes of unsweetened whipped cream.

185 g (6 oz) white chocolate
45 g (1½ oz) unsalted butter
2 egg whites
½ cup (4 fl oz) cream
60 g (2 oz) dark sweet chocolate to decorate

Break the chocolate into small pieces and put in a bowl which will fit over a saucepan, or into a double boiler. Warm over simmering water until melted.

Cut the butter into tiny pieces and add to the chocolate. Stir and, if it doesn't melt, warm again for a minute over the water. Stir lightly and gently until smooth. Beat the whites until they hold soft peaks and fold through. Beat cream until it holds soft peaks, and fold in gently.

Spoon the mixture into tiny moulds, about ½ cup (4 fl oz) size. Chill for 6 hours to mellow and firm.

To decorate, break the dark chocolate into small squares and melt in the same way you melted the white chocolate. Put into a piping bag with a plain writing tube and form a lattice over the top of each mousse by moving it back and forth fairly quickly so it is quite fine. If it is too thick it won't break easily when it sets. Return to chill for 30 minutes.

If covered, this can be kept for 48 hours.

Makes 4 small portions

CHOCOLATE LAYERS FILLED WITH HAZELNUT PRALINE CREAM

A wonderful dessert of soufflé-light chocolate layers alternating with layers of cream, mixed with a crushed hazelnut toffee in between.

You can make the hazelnut praline well ahead, crushing it, and storing it in a jar in the refrigerator. I find it keeps well for weeks, just needing a shake or separating with a fork before it is used. Try to assemble the dessert about 6 hours before serving so there is a blending and mellowing of the flavours.

CHOCOLATE LAYERS

200 g (6½ oz) dark chocolate
2 tbsp strong coffee
5 eggs
⅓ cup caster sugar

Cover 3 flat baking trays with non-stick paper that has been lightly buttered. Draw a circle about the size of a dinner plate, 20 cm (8″), on each one. If you don't have three trays, you can cook the chocolate layers one after another, although the third one will then be a little flatter.

Break the chocolate into pieces and place into a basin or double boiler. Melt standing the basin over a pan of hot water. When softened, add the coffee and stir. Cool until tepid.

Separate the eggs, add the yolks to the chocolate, one at a time, mixing in well. Beat the whites until they are stiff, add the caster sugar and give another beat to dissolve the sugar granules. Fold this into the chocolate mixture, one third first to lighten, then the remainder.

Chocolate Layers Filled with Hazelnut Praline Cream (page 116).

A Small Chocolate Mountain Frosted with Pink (page 122).

Divide between the three trays and spread out evenly inside the circles. The mixture will appear soft, but will hold its shape. Bake each one in a moderate oven (180°C/350°F) for about 18 minutes or until just firm to touch. If the trays are at various levels in the oven, swap the top and bottom ones around halfway through the cooking. Leave to cool for 5 minutes on the tray and then carefully loosen.

The layers are fragile. Turn out carefully onto a piece of fresh non-stick paper and leave to cool.

You can store them for 24 hours in a cake tin with paper or foil between each layer, so they can be easily lifted out.

PRALINE CREAM

60 g (2 oz) hazelnuts, finely chopped
½ cup sugar
¼ cup (2 fl oz) water
1 cup (8 fl oz) cream
a little cocoa for dusting on top of the cakes

Toast the hazelnuts until golden. You can do this on a flat tray in the oven or in a dry frying pan, but stir them occasionally or they don't colour evenly.

Heat the sugar and water in a saucepan until the sugar has dissolved, giving the pan an occasional shake but don't stir. Once it is dissolved turn up the heat and boil rapidly until golden. Add the nuts to this toffee — it will become very thick — return to the heat and cook until it thins again. Stir and watch as it can burn if left. Pour out onto a piece of lightly oiled foil. When cold crush the praline, using a food processor or a meat mallet.

Whip the cream until it holds stiff peaks, fold in the crushed praline.

Put a round of the chocolate cake on a serving plate, top with half the cream and smooth to the edges and then top with a second round of cake. Press down gently and top with the remainder of the cream and the last cake round. Lightly dust the top with sieved cocoa. Refrigerate for at least a couple of hours to mature before serving.

You can assemble this 24 hours ahead — it still tastes wonderful — but the crunchiness of the praline vanishes as it softens, so some of the charm of the contrasts, the rich soft cake and toasted nut and toffee, is gone.

HAZELNUT AND CHOCOLATE TORTE

One of my favourite cakes of this type, beautifully textured and well-flavoured with nuts. I like it left quite plain — don't try and ice this cake — but a little whipped cream on the side is nice. Occasionally, I put a green leaf on the plate with a few berries or segments of orange to make it look prettier.

3/4 cup hazelnuts
90 g (3 oz) dark sweetened eating chocolate
45 g (1½ oz) unsalted butter
1/3 cup caster sugar
2 eggs
few drops vanilla essence

Butter a round deep cake tin, 15 cm (6″) in size. Line the base with non-stick baking paper and butter this too.

Place the hazelnuts on a tray in the oven and heat until the skins are dark and the hazelnuts toasted. (Some health food shops sell them in packets already browned, but be sure they are fresh.) Remove the nuts to a cloth or tea towel and rub until the skins are loosened. Sometimes a little of the dark skin remains but this is fine as long as most comes away. Grind the nuts finely.

Break the chocolate into small squares. Place in a basin and stand over a pan of warm water or in a double boiler until melted. Cream the butter and sugar until light and fluffy. Add the eggs, one at a time. You may find the mixture curdles, but it will smooth out once the chocolate is added. Add the melted chocolate (it must not be too warm) and flavour with vanilla. Fold through nuts and put into the prepared tin.

Bake in a moderate oven (180°C/350°F) for about 25 minutes or until firm on the edges and set, but still a little soft if pressed in the centre. Leave to cool in the tin for about 10 minutes. Run a knife carefully around the edge. Turn out, not onto a cake rack as it is too fragile, but onto a piece of non-stick baking paper. Leave to cool completely; the cake will deflate as it cools.

Serves 6

FUDGE CHOCOLATE TART

Although this looks a bit plain, it tastes wonderful — very fudgey. You could decorate it with some swirls of cream, a scattering of grated chocolate or a few cherries to make it look more festive.

PASTRY

¾ cup flour

1 tbsp icing sugar (confectioner's sugar)

60 g (2 oz) butter

1 egg yolk

Lightly butter a pie dish, 20 cm (8″), or you can use a flan tin. The pastry will be only a very thin layer. You can prepare it in a food processor or by hand. Mix the flour and icing sugar together and chop the butter into a few pieces. Add and blend until crumbly, then mix to a paste with an egg yolk. Wrap in some plastic wrap or waxed paper and rest for 20 minutes. Roll out — it is easiest to use two sheets of waxed paper or plastic wrap — and line the pie tin, pressing it well on the base and sides.

Prick the base and sides and bake in a moderate oven (180°C/350°F) until pale golden. This usually takes about 18–20 minutes.

CHOCOLATE FILLING

2 eggs

2 egg yolks

1 cup sugar

3 tbsp cocoa

125 g (4 oz) ground almonds

½ cup (4 fl oz) cream

Beat the eggs, yolks and sugar until thick. Sift in the cocoa, add the almonds and cream, and stir thoroughly. Pour into the pastry case and bake until firm on the edges but slightly soft and fudgey in the centre. This usually takes around 25 minutes. It does firm more as it cools, and it has a deceptively light-coloured crust on top. It is much darker when cut.

Serves 8–10

Layered Chocolate Mould

Velvety and smooth, layers of different chocolate make a log which is rich without being too much of a taste extravaganza. It is best plain, but if you want to put a little fruit on the side, raspberries are really the only ones which go well.

3 tsp gelatine
1/3 cup water
6 egg yolks
3 tbsp caster sugar
1¼ cups (10 fl oz) cream
90 g (3 oz) dark sweetened chocolate
90 g (3 oz) white chocolate
90 g (3 oz) milk sweetened chocolate
1 cup (8 fl oz) cream

Brush a log tin with a flavourless oil. Mix the gelatine with water and leave aside.

Beat the yolks with the sugar until thick. Heat the cream until almost boiling, then add gradually to the yolks, whisking or stirring. Return to the heat and cook, stirring with a whisk until lightly thickened. Don't let it boil.

Add the gelatine and stir, off the heat, until dissolved.

Divide the custard into three bowls. Cut the three types of chocolate into tiny pieces, or grate them. While the custard is still hot, place the dark chocolate into one bowl, the white into another and the milk chocolate into the third. Stir them to be sure they melt evenly in the custard, and leave to cool completely.

Whip the cream until it holds soft peaks, and fold one third into each bowl.

Spoon one of the chocolate layers into the tin — you can please yourself in which order.
I usually divide the two darker chocolates with the white one. Place the log tin into the freezer so it will set quickly. About 10 minutes is long enough. Spoon on the second layer of chocolate and again put in the freezer. When firm, add the third layer.

Chill the mould in the refrigerator, leaving 12 hours to be sure the layers are quite firm.

Invert onto a plate. It should come out easily but, if not, dip the mould in a little warm water.

Cut into slices; it is much easier if you use a knife dipped in hot water. You can serve it quite plain, which is how I like it, or on a little pool of coffee sauce.

COFFEE SAUCE

¼ cup (2 fl oz) strong coffee
1 tbsp sugar
¼ cup (2 fl oz) cream
1 tbsp cognac or brandy

Mix the coffee with the sugar while it is still warm and stir so it dissolves.

Add the cream. If it is very runny whisk lightly, but it should not be whipped to hold peaks or the sauce won't sit nicely under the mould.

Flavour with cognac or brandy and chill until very cold. This sauce can be made 36 hours ahead and stored in a covered bowl.

This makes only a small quantity of sauce. If you want a generous portion for each serve you can double, but the dish is best with just a small amount.

Serves 10

CHOCOLATE TORRONE

A dessert reminiscent of the French 'turinoise' with which it has some historical links. A torrone is a wickedly rich, buttery chocolate cake in the Italian tradition. Be warned about its rich flavour and cut small portions for serving. It softens quickly, so serve this cake from the refrigerator.

125 g (4 oz) milk chocolate
125 g (4 oz) dark sweetened chocolate
3 tbsp white rum
250 g (8 oz) unsalted butter
2 tbsp icing sugar
2 eggs
90 g (3 oz) ground almonds
15 plain, sweet, commercial biscuits

Brush a log tin, preferably a shallow long one so you will be able to make neat slices, with a flavourless oil. Line the base with foil.

Break the two types of chocolate into squares and put in a bowl. Warm the chocolate in this, over simmering water until melted. Meanwhile, beat the butter until creamy. It will be much easier if you use soft butter.

Add the icing sugar and mix well. Separate the eggs and add the yolks, one at a time. Mix in the ground almonds and the chocolate, a little at a time, but only if it is tepid. (Otherwise it will melt the butter and spoil the finished texture.)

Beat the whites until stiff, and fold into the chocolate mixture. Break the biscuits into small pieces with your fingers, but not too small. There should be little crunchy bits in the chocolate, not soggy crumbs.

Spoon into the prepared tin and smooth the top. Cover with some foil and chill until firm. It takes about 12 hours to set really well. To unmould, just run a knife around the edge and it should come out quite easily. Cut into slices, or you could decorate with a little cream and some frosted violets on top if you want to serve the log whole at the table.

Serves 10–12

Small Chocolate Mountain Frosted with Pink

Dark in colour, moist, and with a slight crunch and the texture of coconut, this is a much-loved dessert. The richness is cut by the pink fruity topping. You may be disappointed the first time you make this because the cake deflates and it looks as if it won't be enough for six people. But with cream it is usually plenty, unless they're particularly greedy guests. When raspberries aren't in season, make the orange cream used to fill the Paris Brest (page 80), decorating with a few wisps of candied orange rind, fresh segments of orange or candied violets.

½ cup desiccated coconut
5 egg whites
6 tbsp caster sugar
2 tbsp cocoa

Lightly oil a mould with a 6-cup capacity. A steam pudding basin or an ovenproof china basin is ideal. The mixture won't come right to the top, but you need to have the edges of the container higher than the chocolate so it doesn't colour too much.

Place the coconut into a dry frying pan and heat, giving it a stir every so often until it is a golden colour. Once the pan heats, watch it, because the coconut can burn quickly. Remove and leave to cool.

Beat the egg whites until stiff, add the sugar a little at a time and beat until quite a stiff meringue.

Add the coconut to the meringue. Sift the cocoa over the top and fold through thoroughly.

Place into the prepared basin and level the top. Put into a container of boiling water which comes about halfway up the sides of the basin and bake in a moderate oven (180°C/350°F) until it is quite firm on top. Timing can vary according to the type of basin used, but as a rule about 35–45 minutes is sufficient. It will be puffed like a soufflé when you take it out but it shrinks as it cools. Leave to stand for about 20 minutes, and then gently turn out onto a plate. It will have shrunk away from the sides a little so it is easy to invert.

Leave to cool completely and, if not decorating immediately, cover and refrigerate. It may shrink even more as it stands for a day, but the texture becomes even nicer.

PINK TOPPING

1 cup (8 fl oz) cream
½ cup fresh or frozen raspberries
1 tsp sugar
185 g (6 oz) fresh raspberries to decorate

Once topped with its pink coating, it is best eaten within 12 hours.

Whisk or beat the cream until it holds firm peaks.

Put the raspberries and sugar into a bowl, stir and crush them lightly with a fork. Leave to stand for about 10 minutes or until some juices form. Push through a sieve into a bowl.

Add the red raspberry juice. Don't stir through completely; it is much prettier if it is marbled. Spoon half over the chocolate and spread out to cover.

Place the remaining pink cream into a piping bag and pipe a trim of rosettes around the base and another row around the top. Either fill the top with fresh raspberries or decorate by placing some around the sides.

Refrigerate for several hours for the flavours to mellow. To serve, cut into slices like a cake. The soft texture makes it easy to cut quite neatly.

Serves 4–6

Decorations and Accompaniments

In earlier times, desserts were always decorated — ornately and extravagantly with vivid, often lurid, colours. Sweets were made in forms of birds and fish. Gilded and glistening, they would be presented like a fanciful tableau at the end of a feast.

Nowadays, we avoid such ostentation, realising a piped rosette of cream with a shaving of curled chocolate on top; a frosted mauve violet or rose petal; tiny wisps of candied peel; or a chocolate ivy leaf, are all that is needed to make a pretty dessert even prettier.

The main thing to remember is to let the decoration reflect in some way the flavouring of the dessert, or it could provide a contrast in texture. The same applies to dessert biscuits, which can provide the perfect accompaniment for fruit desserts and ice-creams. See also Creams, Custards and Sauces (pages 42-47).

Candied violets

The French prepare wonderful year-round reminders of spring: bright purple candied violets. These last at least a year. You can buy them in gourmet shops or, occasionally, in cake shops that sell cake-decorating equipment.

It is possible to make your own. Australian violets are a paler, more mauve shade than the French ones. Fragile in appearance, they make a pretty decoration for chocolate mousse, cakes or desserts. Unfortunately, they have only a short life, keeping about 10 days in an airtight container in a dark cupboard.

Be sure to use violets which have not been sprayed with any chemicals, so they will have the traditional musky flavour associated with this flower. Prepare them as soon as possible after picking.

---

violets
1 egg white
sieved pure icing sugar (confectioner's sugar)
non-stick baking paper

Trim the violets so they have just the tiniest piece of stalk remaining.

Whisk the egg white so it becomes very frothy. Dip each head of violet into the egg white, hold for a few seconds to allow any excess to drip away, and then dip into the sugar. Shake off any excess sugar.

Place the violet upright on the non-stick paper and leave to dry, all day or for 24 hours, depending on the weather.

You can treat rose petals in exactly the same way, but again be careful they have not been sprayed. Choose pink or red ones, which have the most fragrance and flavour and will look very pretty when frosted.

Chocolate leaves

Ivy leaves are the ones most frequently used for this purpose, but small citrus leaves or even firm rose leaves can also be used. Soft leaves are not suitable. Fairly firm leaves are needed to give a base for coating, or they break when you peel the leaf away from the chocolate. Once set, chocolate leaves can be stored in a covered container in the refrigerator for about a week, or for at least a month in the freezer.

90 g (3 oz) dark chocolate | *12 small citrus, ivy, camellia or rose leaves*

Break the chocolate into squares and put into a small bowl. Sit this over a pan filled with hot water. Leave to melt, stirring gently. Wipe the leaves. Spread the chocolate evenly over one side of the leaf: the one with the most distinctive markings. Be careful not to get any on the other side. Place each leaf on a small tray on which you have placed some non-stick paper. If you think the coating is too thin, you can add a second coat when the first is set.

In hot weather leave to firm in the refrigerator, although they will be shinier if left to set at room temperature.

Carefully peel away the leaf from the chocolate and store the chocolate leaves in the refrigerator.

TOFFEE BARK

Wafer thin, with a glassy, marbled appearance, long strips or shreds of this toffee bark can be used to decorate simple dishes of fresh fruits which are served with cream. I find it keeps several weeks in the refrigerator as long as the jar is quite airtight.

foil, about 30 cm by 20 cm (12″ x 8″)
flavourless vegetable oil
½ cup caster sugar
2 tbsp raw sugar

Brush the foil with the flavourless oil and place on a flat baking sheet, oiled side upwards. Put the sugars into a sieve and sift a layer over the top as evenly as you can. Be careful not to make it thick in the centre as this is the last part to colour.

Place into a hot oven, about the centre shelf at 220°C/325°F, and leave for about 5 minutes or until it has melted into a golden sheet. It always becomes too dark on the edges — you have to discard a little of the toffee once cool — but see that the whole sheet doesn't burn.

Remove carefully from the oven. The toffee will be quite thin and running at this stage. Leave on the bench or a rack to cool. Break into thin pieces, long rather than square, and discard any burnt bits. Store in a sealed jar in the refrigerator.

TOFFEE-COATED NUTS

Use these to garnish the top of any cake which has a nut filling, on top of ice-cream or perched on a plain dessert. Any type of nut can be used, provided, of course, it is not salted. If you want to coat almonds, use blanched ones; hazelnuts need toasting so the dark skin can be rubbed away.

½ cup sugar
¼ cup water
nuts

Put the sugar and water into a small saucepan; copper is best if you have it. Leave for 5 minutes to soften the sugar and warm gently, giving the pan an occasional shake. Don't stir. This leaves sugar on the sides, making it easy for the toffee to crystallise. Once the sugar has dissolved, turn up the heat until a golden caramel has formed.

Have the nuts on toothpicks ready to dip. Oil a piece of foil and leave this on the bench. Once the toffee is ready remove from the heat so it won't continue cooking.

Dip each nut into the pan. It is easiest if you tilt it slightly. Hold for a second to let the excess drain away, and then place on the foil. Leave to set. The toffee coating will firm in about 20 minutes. You can store the nuts in a screw top jar in the refrigerator for several weeks without their becoming sticky. Put a little piece of baking paper between the layers of nuts, so you can remove them easily. Be gentle: the toffee casing is thin and brittle so will break if you shake the jar roughly.

Madeleines

A peaked, buttery small cake, associated by most French people with Madeleine, the town in Lorraine that bakes them in huge quantities for sale in other regions. They can be flavoured with lemon, orange, vanilla and occasionally *eau de vie*. French writer Marcel Proust described this fluted cake which seems to have been moulded in a scallop shell as 'plumply sensual beneath its severe and religious folds'.

Arrange madeleines overlapping on a dish, their frosted sugar side uppermost, to accompany poached or fresh fruits, ice-cream or simply a cup of coffee.

Ideally, you need special moulds, available from most gourmet cookware shops, to make these cakes.

2 eggs
60 g (2 oz) sugar
grated rind 1 lemon
60 g (2 oz) flour
½ tsp baking powder
60 g (2 oz) unsalted butter
icing sugar (confectioner's sugar)

Prepare the madeleine tins by buttering them well and then sift flour over to coat. Turn upside down and bang firmly to remove any excess flour. Beat the eggs and sugar together until they are thick and pale, then add the lemon rind. Cut the butter into small pieces, place in a saucepan and leave to melt slowly.

Sift the flour with the baking powder over the top of the egg yolks and fold through very gently. Check that the butter is not hot — it should only be tepid — and fold this carefully into the mixture.

Fill the madeleine moulds almost to the top and bang them gently so there aren't any air bubbles.

Put the moulds into a moderate oven (180°C/350°F) and bake for about 15–18 minutes. They must be firm to the touch on top, a golden colour, and forming a peak in the centre.

Invert the madeleine tins on your bench and bang gently on the edge. All the madeleines should fall out. If any remain give another bang to loosen.

Place them on a cake rack to cool and, before you serve them, dust the top with sifted icing sugar.

Serve on the day they are made.

Almond wafers

The elegant French name for these is Tuiles aux Amandes — which translates rather prosaically as almond tiles. They are so named because they are cooled over a rolling pin so they curve gracefully, like a French tile. Light and crisp, they are a little fragile, so handle carefully. Be sure to store in an airtight tin or they soften quickly.

60 g (2 oz) butter
3 tbsp sugar
3 tbsp flour
¼ tsp vanilla essence
1 large egg white
60 g (2 oz) flaked almonds

Cream the butter with the sugar until light and fluffy. Add the flour and vanilla essence, and mix through the egg white.

Grease a flat baking sheet or tray and scatter lightly with flour. Bang firmly to get rid of any excess flour.

Put four small spoonfuls of the mixture on the tray (use a dessertspoon or ½ tablespoon). You must leave plenty of space for the wafers to spread, so don't crowd on the tray. Using a knife or spatula, spread out to form a flat circle; keep the mixture as evenly thin as possible so it will colour evenly as it cooks. Scatter the top with flaked almonds.

Put into a moderate oven (180°C/350°F) and bake for about 10–12 minutes or until pale brown on the edges and golden in the centre. As soon as you take the tray from the oven you need to remove the wafers or they will set and you won't be able to form into the traditional half-moon shape.

Place each one on a rolling pin, pressing down gently so it fits over and curves and leave to cool. Transfer to a tray and repeat this procedure until they are all cooked. Store in an airtight tin as they soften fairly quickly. Handle them gently, they are quite fragile.

Makes 12

INDEX

BIBLIOGRAPHY

ACTON, ELIZA. *Modern Cookery.* London, 1845.
CHILD, JULIA. *From Julia Child's Kitchen.* Alfred A. Knopf Inc., USA, 1970.
GRIGSON, JANE. *Jane Grigson's Fruit Book.* Michael Joseph, London, 1982.
Harrod's Book of Entertaining. Angus & Robertson, Sydney, 1986.
REMOLIF SHERE, LINDSAY. *Chez Panisse Desserts.* Random House, New York, 1985.
ROOT, WAVERLEY. *Food.* Simon & Shuster, New York, 1980.
SYMONS, MICHAEL. *One Continuous Picnic.* Duck Press. Adelaide, 1982.